Chosen for His People

A Biography of Patriarch Tikhon

by Jane Swan
Preface by Scott M. Kenworthy

T0294125

HOLY TRINITY SEMINARY PRESS
Holy Trinity Monastery
Jordanville, New York

Printed with the blessing of His Eminence,
Metropolitan Hilarion First Hierarch
of the Russian Orthodox Church Outside of Russia

Chosen for His People: A Biography of Patriarch Tikhon, 2nd Edition
© 2015 Holy Trinity Monastery

Second Printing 2023

HOLY TRINITY
SEMINARY PRESS

An imprint of

† HOLY TRINITY PUBLICATIONS
Holy Trinity Monastery
Jordanville, New York 13361-0036
www.holytrinitypublications.com

First Edition: A Biography of Patriarch Tikhon
© 1964 Holy Trinity Monastery

ISBN: 978-1-942699-02-6 (paperback)
ISBN: 978-1-942699-03-3 (ePub)

Library of Congress Control Number: 2015933221

CONTENTS

PREFACE

S t Tikhon (Bellavin, 1865–1925), Patriarch of Moscow and
All Russia from 1917 to 1925, was one of the most important figures in twentieth-century Orthodox Church history.
Moreover, as head of the largest nongovernmental institution
in Russia at the time of one of the twentieth century's pivotal
events—the Russian Revolution—he is a key figure in modern world history. It is a remarkable fact, therefore, that Jane
Swan's book, originally published half a century ago, remains
the only English-language biography. When Swan wrote
her doctoral dissertation at the University of Pennsylvania in
1955, which was published as *A Biography of Patriarch Tikhon*
in Jordanville in 1964, the sources available were quite limited. The main sources that Swan used consisted of émigré
accounts such as those by Metropolitan Anastassy, Archimandrite Constantine (Zaitsev), Protopresbyter Michael Polsky,
and others; and accounts by Western observers, some of whom
(like W. C. Emhardt) were supportive of the Russian Church,
but others, such as Matthew Spinka (professor of church history at Hartford Seminary) and Julius Hecker, tended to
be quite critical of the Church. Swan also utilized primary
sources, especially St Tikhon's own proclamations as well as
Soviet newspaper reports. Not many new sources became
available until the collapse of the Soviet Union.

Since the fall of communism, there has been a burgeon-
ing interest in Russia both in the person of St Tikhon and in
the fate of the Orthodox Church during the Revolution. This,
combined with greater access to archival documents (especially
in the late 1990s), resulted in very significant publications,
including a massive volume of documents gathered by the
secret police (Cheka/GPU) as it prepared the trial against the
patriarch. Russian scholars have also written biographies and
more specialized monographs about St Tikhon or particular aspects of his life, both before and after the Revolution.
It is therefore possible to know much more now than half a
century ago when Swan published her book. It is possible to
answer with much greater certainty long-standing questions,
such as the government's motivations behind the confiscation
of church valuables and involvement in the "Living Church"
schism in 1922, what precipitated the patriarch's change of
course in 1923, and the circumstances around his death and
"last will." All of this requires an entirely new and thorough
investigation.

Nevertheless, Swan's book remains the only biography
available in English, and it has stood the test of time. It is
particularly valuable because it presents in English many of
St Tikhon's key epistles and addresses, as well as documents
from the Soviet side. There are, to be sure, some inaccura-
cies and factual errors, especially about his early life and his
family, which have been indicated in the notes of the current edition. Recent scholarship has not overturned her
key insights, however, but in many cases has strengthened
them. Her presentation of the intent of St Tikhon's harsh
criticisms of the Soviet regime in 1918, for example, is an
important corrective to much western scholarship, which
tended to accept the Soviet accusation that his actions were
"counter-revolutionary"—that is, intended to overthrow the
regime. She also presents a nuanced portrayal of the patriarch
willing to make certain compromises with the Soviet regime

by 1923 in order to preserve the Church from total fragmentation from within, while at the same time not completely capitulating to the demands of the regime. In the former, as in the latter, Swan argues, St Tikhon was guided by the same principle: while not interfering in politics, that the Church and its unity must be protected above all else.

Scott M. Kenworthy
Miami University

CHAPTER I

Years of Preparation

In 1865, the town of Toropets in the province of Pskov was almost untouched by any of the advantages or disadvantages of the modern era. The nearest railroad was 200[1] versts away, and the old traditional Russian ways were still fully maintained. Life was patriarchal in character and slow in tempo. Industry was unknown and the economy of the town was dependent on the agrarian cycle of the surrounding area. Twenty-six years before, Modest Mussorgsky had been born near Toropets, but his fame had not yet trickled back, nor was he ever to bring such glory to the town as the man Vasily Ivanovich Bellavin, who was born January 19, 1865, old style.[2]

The family of Bellavin had long been connected with the Church. Vasily's father was a priest who had spent his entire life at Toropets and, as was the custom, his sons also would be expected to enter the priesthood.[3] Toropets[4] was a town bathed in religious atmosphere. Churches set the keynote. It could be compared to Moscow, for both were ancient, both were primarily religious strongholds and towns only as an afterthought, and both contained famous relics to which pilgrims continually flocked.

Except for the bare outlines of schooling,[5] little is known about the youth of Vasily. He was one of three sons, all of whom lived till manhood. It was just after Vasily became bishop of

Alaska, at the age of thirty-five, that his youngest brother died, and the new bishop accompanied the body back to Toropets for burial. This incident had been predicted many years before by Vasily's father in one of those curiously prophetic dreams that seem to come to people close to the soil. One night the old Bellavin had dreamed that he spoke with his dead mother. The mother warned him of his imminent death and then went on to say that of his three sons, one would be protector,[6] one would die a youth, and one would be brought back to Toropets, and Vasily would become great.

In 1878, Vasily entered the Pskov Seminary. Seminaries in Russia provided free religious training for future priests. Seminary education was usually the end of a priest's formal schooling and was finished when the student was twenty years old. A few of the most brilliant students were elected to continue their studies at one of the four academies[7] in Russia. These men were trained as learned theologians and professors, and often, after taking vows, they became bishops.

Vasily was one of the few selected to enter the Theological Academy at St Petersburg, where he went in 1884 at the age of nineteen. Because the normal age at entrance was twenty years old, his early admission attested to his superior scholastic abilities. From almost the beginning of his studies, his comrades affectionately nicknamed him "Patriarch."[8] The little that has been written about him by his friends speaks of his constant popularity with his colleagues for his gentle ways, complete simplicity, and ever-ready wit. The young Vasily, as well as the later Patriarch Tikhon, had a joke and kind word for everyone.[9]

During his studies at the St Petersburg Academy, the rector dismissed a popular librarian of the academy because of his political leanings. The library belonged completely to the students, being owned, supported, and operated by them.[10] Up to this time, the students had elected the librarian, and consequently, they were incensed over this action of the rector.

So violent were the protests that the students refused to elect a new librarian. The rector appointed Vasily as the new librarian, and given his great popularity, the students ceased protesting and accepted the rector's decision.

In 1888, Vasily finished the St Petersburg Academy still as a layman[11] and returned to the Pskov Seminary as a professor of dogmatic and moral theology. He settled in the town of Pskov, and here his utter lack of material interest soon showed itself by the manner in which he lived. His home was a tiny annex to a simple wooden house near the church of St Nicholas, but such simplicity of life only further endeared him to his friends. Between 1888 and 1891, he continued teaching at the Pskov Seminary, and it was only in 1891 that he took vows to enter monastic life. The ceremony took place on the second floor of a church, and so great was the rush of people that special supports for the ceiling had to be added quickly, to bear the weight of the people. Thus at the age of twenty-six, Vasily Ivanovich Bellavin became the Russian Orthodox monk Tikhon.[12]

From the Pskov Seminary, Tikhon, in March 1892, was transferred to a seminary in Kholm, in the province of Lublin in Poland, where he was made inspector. From the Kholm Seminary, Tikhon was for a short time transferred to the Kazan Theological Seminary as rector with the rank of archimandrite,[13] but he soon returned to the Kholm Seminary having been made rector.

Metropolitan Evlogy, who was a teacher in the seminary at that time, gave a detailed account of Tikhon's work during his five-year rectorship at the Kholm Seminary. Tikhon introduced literary and musical meetings, which took place once a week on a weekday evening and every Sunday after the morning services. Lectures, discussions, and concerts were presented, and the public was invited. After each meeting, the rector invited all for tea. Almost immediately after he was appointed, he had a new second chapel erected at the seminary in memory of the finding of the relics of

Theodosius of Chernigov. A daily service was held at the new chapel, and each day one of the six classes did the singing. The local elementary-school children were invited to perform on holidays. Such methods ensured his immediate popularity, and soon he was invited to serve at all the local churches. This serving at other churches became part of Tikhon's work throughout his life, and the enormous demands made on him, no matter where he went, attest to his popularity.

Kholm, by history and tradition, was one of the sorest spots for the Church authorities. The town was composed chiefly of Roman Catholics constantly at odds with the Orthodox and a large proportion of Uniates,[14] who were considered as potential Orthodox converts.[15] Throughout the ages, constant friction has existed among the three groups. Tikhon, with his gentle unprovocative ways, was an excellent person to be placed in such a position, and he quickly became popular with all groups. So successful was he in allaying suspicion and hostility that Archbishop Flavian chose him to be his personal assistant. Under his tactful administration, many Uniates returned to the Orthodox confession.

Reports of his successful work reached the Synod, and a movement began to make him a bishop. By canon law, however, no monk can become bishop until he is thirty-three years old, but in this case, the Synod made an exception and consecrated him bishop of Lublin on October 19, 1897.[16] After the consecration, he returned to Kholm for a year as vicar bishop[17] of the Kholm Diocese.

On September 14, 1898, Tikhon was made bishop of the Aleutian Islands and Alaska,[18] whose diocesan see was located in San Francisco. From 1899 to 1907, he remained in the United States with only one quick trip to Russia in those eight years.

When the news reached people in Kholm that their bishop was being transferred to an independent see of his own, riots broke out. He was forced to hold farewell services in each individual church, and street fighting occurred in an attempt to stop him from going. On the day of his actual departure, people threw themselves on the tracks to keep the train from leaving and had to be removed forcibly.

While Bishop Tikhon was en route to his new see, his young brother, who was accompanying him, died. Tikhon took the body back to Toropets for burial, thus fulfilling his father's dream.[19]

Tikhon's years in the United States were not only extremely productive, as far as successful administration of his diocese was concerned, but for Tikhon personally, they were years of useful experience that served him well later on. Later in life, he mentioned the fact that his U.S. sojourn widened not only his ecclesiastical horizon but also his political outlook.[20]

In all the recorded sermons and speeches, there is seldom any personal reference. Early in life, in his manner of living, and in his dealings with people, he completely effaced all thought of self. It is only in his first sermon in America, and perhaps because of his recent sad visit to Toropets with the body of his brother,[21] that we find a reference to "my old mother in Russia." Only through this comment has it been possible to establish the fact that his mother survived the father and lived to see the four boys grown to manhood.[22]

In 1905, because of the great increase of Orthodox parishes in America, chiefly under Tikhon's guidance, the American Mission was made into an archdiocese, and Tikhon was promoted to the rank of archbishop at the age of forty. The diocese was divided into two vicariates, one located in Alaska and one in Brooklyn, New York. A cathedral was built and completed in New York City on 97th Street, and the official see was removed there. Along with the St Nicholas Cathedral in New York, Tikhon established a theological seminary[23] in Minneapolis, Minnesota, and the St Tikhon's Monastery in South Canaan, Pennsylvania. The number of parishes increased from fifteen to seventy in the United States, and all the parishes became self-supporting.

Again, as in Kholm, Tikhon continued his missionary activities[24] among the Uniates, and a large number returned to the Orthodox confession.[25]

Although the renowned Konstantin Pobedonostsev was still chief procurator of the Holy Synod, Tikhon was called back from America only once to be a member of the Synod.[26] As soon as the session was over, he returned to America and stayed until he was transferred to Yaroslavl' on January 25, 1907.

Tikhon's actions in Yaroslavl' at first created only amazement. He never refused to serve in the churches, monasteries, or even the smallest village parish churches. He constantly made trips to churches without any pomp or ceremony, examined minutely all the affairs of the church, and even climbed up to the church belfries[27] to see the bells. Amazement soon turned to love, for with high and low, he maintained the same friendly manner, usually speaking kindly and always ready with a joke. Parish priests soon came to expect the archbishop at any time, arriving on foot without fanfare, examining books, discussing local problems, and remaining quick to notice all the details of the provincial church life.

In 1913, Tikhon[28] was appointed archbishop of Vilnius and had to leave Yaroslavl'. The entire province was saddened, and at a grand farewell ceremony, he was made an honorary citizen of the city, the first time any bishop was ever so honored.

It was in Vilnius that Tikhon's former work with Roman Catholics and Uniates both in Kholm and in the United States stood him in good stead. The Vilnius Diocese was composed largely of Roman Catholics and Uniates. A further complication was the strong historical animosity existing between the Russian Orthodox and the Polish population. Here, the church was forced to display more pomp and ceremony to appeal to the Polish temperament, and such a role was difficult for a man of Tikhon's character. The local Polish population were chiefly members of the intelligentsia, quick to criticize and quick to be offended. The majority of them were Catholics and deeply distrustful of Russian Orthodoxy. Tikhon was unable to maintain the necessary formality while conducting services, but he then would shock many by being driven to the magnificent summer home for the archbishop in a simple carriage with only a small cap on his head. Around Trynopol, where the archbishop's home was located, was a section known as Calvary, which consisted of a series of Roman Catholic chapels marking the stations of the cross. Here it was Tikhon's wont to walk dressed only in the plain monk's frock and cap. Soon, the familiar figure was greeted on all sides by the Catholic priests and peasants, Jews, and Uniates, and a growing respect and liking grew up for the cheerful archbishop. However, this slow and constructive work of allaying distrust and building up united foundations, free of national and religious dissension, was soon interrupted by the outbreak of the World War I. Vilnius soon became a center of war activities, and within a few months the frontline passed over it.

At first, all the secular and religious institutions were removed to Moscow, and here Tikhon was transferred, bringing with him the most valuable of the church vessels and holy relics, but this proved too far from his diocese, so Tikhon moved to Dzisna, which was on the edge of the Vilnius Diocese.

From here Tikhon carried on extensive war work. His activities were at first with the refugees, but gradually they came to be centered with the soldiers at the front. He visited the front personally, conducted services, was caught under bombardment, and did such splendid work maintaining the morale of the soldiers that he was awarded a military order with swords for distinguished conduct.

During these war years, he frequently was called on to attend meetings of the Synod, and in December 1915 he was sent to Tobolsk to investigate the complex affair of Bishop Varnava's local glorification of St John of Tobolsk, which was not sanctioned by the Synod. After the February Revolution of 1917, in March of that year, Vladimir L'vov became chief procurator of the Holy Synod. In the first meeting in March 1917, at his suggestion, a Synod appeal was issued, which spoke of the Revolution as the "will of God"[29] and begged that all dissentions should be set aside, all quarrels ended, and the war successfully persecuted under the Provisional Government, which would work for the good of Russia. Prayers were changed, and mention of the emperor was replaced by the "right-believing Provisional Government." Friction became so strong that L'vov—asserting his power as chief procurator—dismissed the Synod in April 1917 and called a new one, which retained only two old members, Archbishop Sergius (Stragorodsky) of Vladimir and Archbishop Platon (Rozhdestvensky), Exarch of Georgia.

With the abdication of the tsar, a period of ecclesiastical revolutionary activity swept up some of the lower clergy who were eager to settle scores with unpopular bishops. Things became so chaotic that the Synod adopted a rule declaring that the bishop should be elected by the clergy and laymen of the diocese. In actual fact, most bishops were reelected, but although Moscow had been sent Bishop Joasaph by Synod[30] appointment to replace Metropolitan Makary (Nevsky), who was dismissed by L'vov, the people of Moscow decided to elect their own metropolitan. A delegation of clergy and laymen were sent to Petrograd to investigate the records of possible candidates and departed with a long list. Tikhon was almost an unknown personality to the Moscow people, so it was a complete surprise to all when he received the highest number of ballots at the official election,[31] which was held before the miraculous Vladimir icon of the Virgin in the Dormition Cathedral in Moscow.

Almost immediately, it became known that the new metropolitan would officiate in any church, so he was besieged on all sides with invitations. To the great amazement of all, when the service was over, Tikhon gladly visited the parishioners in their homes, no matter how small or humble they might be. Soon, his black-clad figure became a familiar sight to the Moscow citizens, and official reverence was replaced with warm personal love.

CHAPTER 2

Revival of the Patriarchate

The decision to call an All-Russian Council had been taken by Emperor Nicholas II after the Revolution of 1905–1906. Serious preparatory work was accomplished. The question of the restoration of the patriarchate seemed to become the central subject of the council. After the Revolution of 1917, the restoration of the patriarchate became imminent. A special committee was formed to prepare the election of the council and to make all the necessary arrangements.

The new metropolitan of Moscow was a member of this committee and was specifically charged with arranging the reception and housing of all the members who would attend the council. More than sixty bishops were expected, and Tikhon personally visited all the nearby monasteries and checked the accommodations. He also decided where the various meetings were to be held and which churches would be used. It was not until late July 1917 that the elections began, for the actual request for voting was not issued until July 15. Two clergy delegates and three laymen were selected from each diocese by indirect elections. Delegates also were sent from some monasteries, the four academies, military corps, and universities. Additionally, all bishops who were members of the preconciliar committee were considered ex-officio members.[1]

The Composition of the Moscow Council of 1917–1918

There were 564 delegates in all, including the preconciliar committee members who were considered ex-officio members. There were 265 clerics and 299 laymen composed as follows:

Clergy (by rank)		Laity (by occupation)	
10	metropolitans	14	active military
17	archbishops	20	State Duma and State Council members
53	bishops	8	merchants
2	protopresbyters	33	peasants and farmers
15	archimandrites	2	Cossacks
2	igumens	12	delegates of theological academies
3	hieromonks	13	delegates from the Academy of Sciences and universities
5	mitered archpriests	42	government officials and civil servants
67	archpriests	22	lawyers and court officials
55	priests	133	others
2	protodeacons		
8	deacons		
26	psaltists		

On August 11, the Provisional Government gave the coming council the right to work out a new form of church government that was to be submitted to the Ministry of Confessions for approval. On August 16, the council was opened with a solemn service, and various messages—chiefly relating to the chaos of the time—were read by Metropolitan Tikhon; S. K. Rodionov, representing the Moscow Zemstvo; M. V. Rodzianko, former speaker of the Duma; Archpriest Pavel Lakhostsky; and others. By a vote of 407 to 33, Metropolitan Tikhon was elected president of the council, and throughout the meetings, he faithfully presided, often under most trying circumstances.

The main problem before the council was the question of reviving the patriarchate. The complete list of patriarchs up to 1700 is as follows:

St Job	January 26, 1589–June 19, 1607 (removed in June 1605)
St Hermogen	July 3, 1606–February 17, 1612
Philaret	June 24, 1619–October 1, 1633
Joasaph I	January 1634–November 28, 1649
Joseph	March 27, 1642–April 15, 1652
Nikon	July 25, 1652–December 12, 1666 (left office in 1659)
Joasaph II	January 31, 1667–February 17, 1672
Pitirim	July 7, 1672–April 19, 1673
Joachim	July 26, 1674–March 17, 1690
Adrian	August 24, 1690–October 2, 1700
After the death of Patriarch Adrian, Metropolitan Stephan (Yavorsky) served as Patriarchal Locum Tenens until the patriarchate was abolished in 1721.	

The consensus of opinion was for such a revival for many reasons. Some saw it as the only salvation for the future of Russia, and these individuals cited past incidents[2] in Russian history as examples. Others believed that only with a strong religious leader could the Russian people forget their quarrels and return to the old traditional ways.[3] Still others thought of it as a temporary bridge to a monarchy, and a few envisaged a new strong church rising above the ruins of the old political system and rebuilding the House of God rather than the house of man. Only a very few of the 1905 revolutionaries were against it, and although they spoke out strongly, it made almost no impression on the council.[4] Bishop Mitrofan of the Don officially introduced the project on September 11, but discussion was postponed until October 14.

From October 14 to 25, the discussion of the proposal took place. Then on October 25, the Provisional Government was overthrown. On October 28, when the council again met, there was street fighting in Moscow. Metropolitan Tikhon celebrated a solemn prayer service (moleben) for peace, and then he suggested that, in view of the crisis, the debate be stopped and a vote taken. The opposition, however, insisted on the continuation of the discussions. Speeches continued until October 30, at which time Tikhon again suggested a vote. Fighting continued in the streets, and the very existence of the council was precarious. When queried about the number in attendance, Tikhon mistakenly estimated that there was a quorum and referred to former elections of patriarchs when as few as 220 votes had been cast. The actual proposal to elect a patriarch was carried by 141 votes against 112, with 12 abstaining. Actually this was less then half of the original council members, and therefore no quorum, and only one-quarter of the members carried the responsibility of the decision. Because there was no objection when the later voting took place, it is reasonably certain that the absent members must have been satisfied with the decision.

Along with the decision to restore the patriarchate, the respective spheres of power were worked out. On November 4, it was ruled that the supreme authority, legislative, administrative, judicial, and supervisory, belonged to the council, which was to meet periodically, but the patriarch was to head the ecclesiastical administration in the interim periods, being responsible to the council when it met. The patriarch was to be first among bishops of equal rank, but the bishops were equal to him.

During the last excited days of October, a constant bombardment was ensuing in the streets. The main target was the Kremlin, where a group of young cadets had entrenched themselves and were making a last-ditch stand. An appeal was made by the council to the Military Revolutionary Committee to cease fighting, for great concern was felt over the holy places of the Kremlin, which in fact, suffered severely from artillery fire.[5] Tikhon, at the head of a committee from the council, went to the Kremlin during the actual fighting. So frightful was the carnage that all but two of the committee turned back, and the council was in an uproar, fearing for the lives of the churchmen. Tikhon ascertained the damage to the Kremlin and came back to report to the council. A plan was made for an enormous procession (*krestniy khod*)[6] around the fighting area to stop the bloodshed, but the fighting ended almost immediately afterward, on November 4.

On October 31, candidate nominations took place after the decision had been made that the election of the patriarch was to follow the historical pattern used in the seventeenth century. On the first ballot,[7] Archbishop Antony of Kharkov received 101 votes. Archbishop Arseny of Novgorod was second with 27 votes, and Metropolitan Tikhon was third with 23 votes. On the second ballot, only the top three contenders were considered. Archbishop Antony got 159 votes, four more than needed for nomination, whereas Archbishop Arseny got 148 votes and Metropolitan Tikhon received 125 votes. On the third ballot, Arseny received enough votes for nomination, but it was not until the fourth ballot that Tikhon got the necessary number to be one of the nominees.[8]

The names of the three officially nominated candidates were placed on separate slips of paper, set in a blessed urn, and put before the most famous of all Russian icons, the Vladimir icon of the Theotokos.[9] The icon had been moved from its usual spot[10] in the Dormition Cathedral to the Cathedral of Christ the Saviour for this ceremony. All night, the urn remained before the icon dimly lit by flickering candles. The following morning, Metropolitan Vladimir[11] celebrated a long and solemn liturgy before the icon. Then, by a prearranged choice, staretz[12] Alexis (Soloviev) of Zosimov Monastery[13] drew out one of the names. Turning to Metropolitan Vladimir, the staretz handed him the slip, and the metropolitan crossing himself read out, "Tikhon, Metropolitan of Moscow, Axios!"[14]

Like a spark igniting dry wood, the entire church was filled with shouts of "Axios, Axios!" Above it all, the choir intoned, "We praise thee, O Lord."

At the end of the service, amid pandemonium, the bishops filed out of the church. Suddenly, from among the milling crowds, part of which were obviously hostile to the event that had just taken place, a half-insane woman with long flowing hair rushed up to Archbishop Evlogy and shouted: "Not long, not long will you celebrate! Soon your bishop will be murdered."[15]

During the actual drawing of the name, Tikhon had remained at the Moscow podvorye (representation church) of the Trinity–St Sergius Lavra, and a delegation headed by Metropolitan Vladimir was sent to inform him that he had been chosen patriarch of all Russia. On hearing the news, Tikhon at once took a binding vow to defend the Holy Orthodox Russian Church until his death. Tikhon's informal acceptance speech to the delegation gives a very clear picture of Tikhon, the man. Fortunately, a copy of this still exists as it is one of Tikhon's very few recorded talks. He seldom wrote out his speeches, preferring to speak extemporaneously, and left no dogmatic writings or papers other than a few official documents. Following is the speech:

Beloved in Christ, fathers and brethren;

I have just uttered the prescribed words: "I thank and accept and say nothing against." Of course, enormous is my gratitude to the Lord for the mercy bestowed on me. Great also is my gratitude to the members of the Sacred All-Russian Council for the high honor of my election into the members of candidates for the Patriarchate. But arguing, as a man, I could say a lot against my present election. Your news about my election for the Patriarchate is to me that scroll on which was written, "Weeping, sighing, and sorrow," which scroll had to be eaten by the prophet Ezekiel (2:10, 3:1).

How many tears will I have to swallow or how many sighs emit in my forthcoming Patriarchal office and especially in the present woeful time. Like the ancient leader of the Hebrews, Moses, I shall have to say to the Lord:

"Wherefore hast thou afflicted thy servant? and wherefore have I not found favour in thy sight, that thou layest the burden of all this people upon me? Have I conceived all this people? Have I begotten them, that thou shouldest say unto me, Carry them in thy bosom, as a nursing father beareth the sucking child ... I am not able to bear all this people alone, because it is too heavy for me" (Numbers 11:11–14).

From now on I am entrusted with the care for all the Russian churches, and what awaits me is the gradual dying for them all my days. Who is content with this even amongst those who are firmer than I? But let the will of the Lord be done, I am strengthened by the fact that I have not sought this election. It came to me without my wish, even without the wish of men, according to the lot of God. I trust that the Lord who had called me, will Himself help me by His all-powerful grace to carry the burden which is placed on me and will make it a light burden. Let it be a comfort and encouragement for me that my election occurs not without the wish of the most pure Theotokos. Twice she, by the coming of her precious Vladimir icon in the Cathedral of Christ the Saviour, was present at my election. This time the lot itself has been taken from her miracle-working icon. It is as if I were placing myself under her high protection. May she, the all powerful, stretch out to me, who is so weak, the hand of her support and may she deliver this city and the whole Russian land from all need and sorrow.[16]

Throughout his whole life, Tikhon made frequent references to his veneration for the Virgin Mary and felt that he had placed himself in her keeping. In this acceptance speech based on quotations from Ezekiel and Numbers, he sincerely mourned that he had been elected, feeling that he had not the strength to bear such a cross, but then, with a "God's will be done," he referred to the twofold intervention of the Virgin Mary in his life through her miraculous Vladimir icon. The original elevation of Tikhon to metropolitan of Moscow, done by the revolutionary method of election rather than by Synod appointment, had been done before the Vladimir icon in the Dormition Cathedral. Now again, when the actual patriarchal lot had been drawn as it were from the icon itself, he was again chosen against his own personal will, so he viewed it as divine intervention and humbly bowed to the will of God.

That Tikhon should take such a view of the situation is not surprising, for certainly the original voting would seem to indicate that the council had desired the strength and fighting qualities of a man like Archbishop Antony or even Arseny, while Tikhon quite obviously was viewed as too mild and retiring for such a controversial position. Nevertheless, the election of Tikhon was accepted by all,[17] and immediate preparations were begun for the installation ceremony. A committee was appointed by the council, headed by Metropolitan Platon, who with two laymen had to seek permission from the Military Revolutionary Committee to neutralize the Kremlin and to celebrate the ceremony of installation in the Dormition Cathedral. On November 8, Metropolitan Platon reported to the council that permission had been granted and that immediate research must be done to determine how the ceremony traditionally had been performed. The service of enthronement was worked out and actual implements of former enthronements were resurrected from the Kremlin. Oddly enough, the seventeenth-century kukol[18] and mantle of Patriarch Nikon fitted Tikhon without alteration. The old patriarchal throne[19] of the Dormition Cathedral was used, and the ancient staff of Metropolitan Peter of Moscow was handed to Tikhon when it was time for his sermon.[20]

During this time of preparation, Metropolitan Tikhon went to the Trinity–St Sergius Lavra to prepare himself spiritually for the coming burdens. The council continued its work, but without the new patriarch as chairman. A public funeral service was held for the killed cadets in the Kremlin and then, because of so many requests by relatives of the men who were killed on the Communist side, the council also conducted a public funeral for the dead Bolsheviks. This, as the council stated, was to comfort the relatives of those misguided soldiers. The new government took no part in either funeral.

On November 21, 1917, amid the ringing of the famous bells of Ivan the Great,[21] Vasily Ivanovich Bellavin was enthroned as the Most Holy Tikhon, patriarch of all Russia, in the Dormition Cathedral. When the ceremony was completed and the liturgy performed, the first and second metropolitans conducted him to the patriarchal throne. There Metropolitan Vladimir, soon to be murdered by the Communists, presented him with the staff of Metropolitan Peter of Moscow, and the new patriarch preached his first sermon.

It is precisely at the greatest moment in his life that Tikhon's humble yet strong conviction of the Virgin Mary's guidance gave him such joy. He delighted in the fact that the installation ceremony was on the feast when the Virgin was presented in the Temple and likened the strangeness of a young girl penetrating into the holy of holies to the equally unbelievable restoration of the patriarchate. He saw the restoration at such a time as a sign of the Lord's mercy to the poverty of spirit of the Russian realm and then came out with a warning to those who were unfaithful and disobedient. He lamented the destruction of holy places, the sons of Russia who had forgotten God's commandments, and yet, heeding God's words, said that the Church would not desert the strayed lambs but would tend them, seek them out, and return them to the ways of righteousness. Clothing his words in the special vocabulary of the Church, Tikhon laid out the path he followed throughout the rest of his life both as patriarch and as a man.[22]

At the end of the sermon, an enormous procession was formed of the clergy and people, and it wound its way around the Kremlin. On all sides, the people knelt to receive the patriarchal blessing. During the entire ceremony, Bolshevik soldiers had been guarding the Dormition Cathedral and were attracting attention by laughing and smoking contemptuously. As the clergy came out of the church, the people surrounding them formed a barrier between the clergy and the soldiers. With the appearance of the clergy carrying icons and banners, the laughing grew more boisterous, but as the blue velvet mantle of Nikon covering the patriarch's shoulders appeared through the crowd, all grew silent. Suddenly one, then two, then all the soldiers broke through the protective barrier of the faithful and threw themselves at the feet of Tikhon, completely blocking his passage. Only when the patriarch had blessed them many times would they open the way for the procession and join in the slow-moving line of people joyously following the patriarch.[23]

What was this man, Vasily Ivanovich Bellavin, like? At the early age of fifty-two, he was called on to bear the responsibilities of the only institution surviving a bloody revolution. Yet the fact of survival was still precarious, for attacks from all sides already had begun. Although his very life was in constant danger, this was probably the least of Tikhon's worries, for on numerous occasions, he showed a complete lack of interest in his own safety. The safety and continuation of the Church to which he was wedded, however, became a burden that he never afterward forgot. That he was fully aware of this burden is shown by his acceptance speech to the delegation at the Holy Trinity podvorye in Moscow. What character traits armed him for this position of almost unbearable responsibilities?

One main trait that always is mentioned in the few accounts[24] of those who knew him personally was his real humility. In examining the few extant writings attributable to the patriarch, only one reference was made to anything personal, that is, the previously mentioned remark about his old mother. It is impossible to find out the man's likes and dislikes, friends, family, interests, or habits from anything he said or wrote. A typical incident was recorded by Metropolitan Anastassy,[25] who knew Tikhon personally and worked in the Synod with him. He recalled that during the 1917 council, Tikhon had as guests staying with him Metropolitan Agathangel,[26] Archbishop Arseny of Novgorod, and Metropolitan Vladimir of Kiev. Vladimir of Kiev was highest in rank and as such was first at the table and given the best room. After Tikhon became patriarch, he insisted that Vladimir retain the same privileges and refused to outrank him in protocol.[27] If one is familiar with the ceremony of the Eastern churches, one can appreciate what a surprising attitude Tikhon here showed. The simplicity with which Tikhon lived, the lack of attendants during his travels, the difficulty he had in displaying pomp even when called on to do so, as in Poland, reveal the innate humility and disregard of self that he demonstrated throughout his entire life.

Tikhon's very mildness and gentleness were misleading on first acquaintance, and many took it for weakness. His enemies have tried to paint him as an ornate figurehead, although their arguments do not hold up when faced with the facts. He could be extremely stubborn in both small and great things. A later description of his dealings not only with the Bolsheviks but also with the Church Synod meetings will fully reveal his strength of character, but the following anecdote demonstrates his strong-mindedness even in a small matter.

During his five years of rectorship at Kholm, an unpleasant situation came to a head concerning teacher's lodgings. Originally, when the student body had numbered only seventy-five, one section of the dormitory had been turned over to the

teachers as living quarters without payment of rent. The Kholm
Seminary was the only seminary in Russia where such a priv-
ilege had been extended to teachers. With the ensuing years,
however, the student body had more than doubled, and the
housing of students was woefully inadequate. Along with the
increased overcrowding of students, the teachers began to turn
their quarters into slums. Nursemaids, cooks, and servants, all
were brought in to live in already overcrowded quarters; children had room to play only in the halls and on the stairway, and
the quarrelling and noise raised a continual din in the seminary.
Gently but steadily, the rector induced one wife after another
to insist that her husband move into town, and by constant per-
suasion, the rector succeeded in clearing the entire dormitory
and turning it over to the students.[28]

Frequent reference has been made to Tikhon's ever-ready
sense of humor even under the most trying experiences. Perhaps this was one of his most endearing qualities to those who
surrounded him, for there was little to relieve the constant tension of the threats and attacks from the Bolsheviks. One of his
visitors who had an audience late in 1924, soon after the patriarch had seen his oldest and dearest friend, his cell-attendant
Yakov Polozov, killed by the shot that was meant for him,
said that the patriarch still had the courage to laugh and cheer
those who came to him for comfort. She spoke to him of her
troubles. Her story was the same one of persecution, famine,
loss of dear ones, which he must have heard hundreds of times
before. He comforted her and then, as she was about to leave,
she suddenly remembered she had brought a picture of him.
Without thinking, she asked for his autograph and the patriarch with a quick smile said. "But I am illiterate—I cannot
sign my name." A moment later he acceded to her request,
and she carried away with her not only comfort but also the
memory of a short moment of fun in her dreary life.[29]

Tikhon's appearance was a very Russian one. He is
described as tall and blonde.[30] His hair had a tendency to curl,

and the most striking feature of his face was his deep-set, very blue eyes. His photographs, all taken after he became patriarch, show a man with a kindly face, a large broad Slavic nose, and a shorter beard than one is accustomed to seeing on the Russian clergy. Although he died at the early age of sixty, his pictures show that he was aged far beyond his years and extremely careworn. That he suffered greatly is obvious, and in the photograph taken of him at his death, he looks like a man of ninety who died in great agony.

CHAPTER 3

1917 to the Famine

After the selection and enthronement of the patriarch, a complete reorganization of Church administration was accomplished. The supreme legislative, administrative, judicial, and supervisory authority belonged to the council, which was to meet periodically and consisted of bishops, clergy, and laymen. The patriarch was to hold first place among bishops of equal rank, but he, with the other organs of Church administration, was subject to the council. His role was similar to a chief executive who convoked the council and presided at their sessions, but during the intervening time, he governed with two elective committees of the council that were also responsible to it for their actions. The patriarch was president of both of the committees, the Holy Synod, and the Supreme Ecclesiastical Council and had veto power over their decisions, even having the power to act independently of them, all subject to the judgment of the next council.

The patriarch's main duties were supervising episcopal appointments, although he did not personally appoint the bishops; checking on the personal and business lives of the bishops and advising on all problems; settling episcopal disputes with recourse to the Synod if his advice was ignored; acting as diocesan bishop[1] for the diocese of Moscow and the stavropegial[2] monasteries; and, most important, fulfilling the unpalatable duty of making protests to the government against encroachments or belligerent actions.

To ensure the final and supreme authority of the council over the patriarch, the following provisions were made:

8. If the Patriarch fails to fulfill his duties, depending on the nature of this transgression, the three senior members of the Holy Synod or the hierarchs who are members of the Supreme Council of the Church give the Patriarch a fraternal warning; if this does not produce results, they give him a second warning; if this second warning goes unheeded, they will take the appropriate measures such as indicated in article 10.

9. The complaints against the Patriarch are presented to the Holy Synod through the hierarch who is senior among the members of the Synod.

10. In the case of the transgression by the Patriarch of the rights and duties of his ministry, a joint session of the Holy Synod and the Supreme Council of the Church resolves whether the Patriarch should be held accountable for his actions. However, the commitment of the Patriarch for the judgment and judgment itself are carried out by the All-Russian Council of Bishops to which, if possible, other Patriarchs and primates of autocephalous churches are invited. The decision to commit the Patriarch for the judgment and the sentence of conviction require a majority of at least two thirds of the votes of those present.[3]

Of the two organs aiding the patriarch in his work when the council was not in session, the Holy Synod consisted of the president-patriarch and twelve bishops, partly chosen by the council and partly dependent on which bishops were in charge of certain key sees. The Holy Synod was chiefly concerned with the inner-organizational problems of the Church, such as administration, doctrine, liturgy, priestly and parochial education, discipline, supervision of missionary enterprises, and censorship of religious books.

The Supreme Ecclesiastical Council consisted of the president-patriarch and fifteen members selected by patriarch and Synod from both higher and lower clergy and laymen. Their work was more external, for example, administrative, economics, finances, the business end of the synodal press, direction of academies, and legal aspects of church life. Matters could be initiated by any member of either body, and often both bodies met jointly.

Although the Bolsheviks had seized power on November 7, the council had been allowed to continue its work. It is true that it was obliged to seek permission to use the Dormition Cathedral for the installation of the patriarch; however, the election of Tikhon and the reorganization of the Church administration were carried without any government interference. Throughout the month of November, the Council of People's Commissars watched the completion of the elections for the Constituent Assembly and consolidated their hold in Petrograd and Moscow. The lull was short-lived, however, and the program, so belligerently proclaimed by the Bolsheviks long before they achieved power, began to take shape.

On December 4, a decree was issued declaring all land was to be taken from private ownership and become part of a national land fund to be controlled by special land committees. This law specifically named ecclesiastical and monastic institutions to be considered within this category. With one blow, the Church lost the greater source of its income, but this was only the first of a long series of equally crippling blows delivered by the new government.[4]

One week later, on December 11, the land nationalization law was succeeded by a decree from the Commissariat of National Education, which stated that all schools whatsoever were to be turned over to this department.[5] It is true that on June 20, 1917, the Provisional Government had taken over parochial schools and ecclesiastical institutions for teachers that had been supported by state funds. The December law, however, made no distinction between Church-supported schools and state-supported schools and even included seminaries and the four academies. This law, carried into practice, meant that the Church had no means of educating young people, not even for the priesthood. A warning afterthought was appended to this decree, stating that the question of churches would be defined in connection with the decree of separation of church from state. Because this decree had not yet been issued, the implied warning shook the council completely.

Again, just one week later, on December 18, a decree was issued stating that the Russian republic recognized only civil marriages. Births and deaths were no longer to be registered by ecclesiastical authorities,[6] but by newly created government bureaus. The recording books and registers possessed by the Church were all to be turned over to the government bureaus, and marriages by ecclesiastical authority would have no civil recognition. This action was followed by taking divorce proceedings out of the hands of ecclesiastics and turning them over to the civil administration.[7]

Early in January 1918, a decree came out that stopped all financial aid for purposes of religious worship and declared all priests' and catechists' salaries would be discontinued after March 1, 1918.[8]

The final blow was published on January 23, 1918, concerning the separation of church and state and the separation of school and church. The decree caused such a change in the life of both the church and state, and their relations with one another, that it is safe to say not one person was unaffected by it throughout the length and breadth of Russia. The entire reorganization of church life was forced by the decree and by it the entire reorganization of man's relation with his church. This document was first published in all the newspapers as "Freedom of Conscience and of Religious Societies," but later it was incorporated into the "Collected Laws of 1918," under the title of "Separation of the Church from the State and the School from the Church."

1. The church is separated from the state.

2. Within the confines of the Republic it is prohibited to issue any local laws or regulations restricting or limiting freedom of conscience, or establishing privileges or preferential rights of any kind based upon the religious affiliation of the citizens.

3. Every citizen may profess any religion or none. All restrictions of rights connected with the profession of any faith whatsoever or with the nonprofession of any faith at all, are annulled.

Note: All reference to the religious affiliation of the citizens, or to the lack thereof, shall be removed from all official documents.

4. The governmental functions, or those of other public and legal institutions, shall not be accompanied by any religious rites or ceremonies.

5. A free performance of religious rites is guaranteed as long as it does not interfere with public order or infringe upon the rights of the citizens of the Soviet Republic. Local authorities possess the right in such cases to adopt all necessary measures to preserve public order and safety.

6. No one may refuse to perform his civil duties on account of his religious views.

Exception to this rule, on condition that one civil duty be exchanged for another, may be granted in each individual case by decision of the People's Court.

7. Religious vows and oaths are abrogated. Only a solemn promise can be given when it is necessary.

8. Acts of civil nature are registered solely by the civil authorities, the departments for the registration of marriages and births.

9. The school is separated from the church. Instruction in religious doctrines is not permitted in any state and public schools, nor in private teaching institutions where general subjects are taught. Citizens may give or receive religious instruction in a private manner.

10. All ecclesiastical or religious associations are subject to the general regulations regarding private associations and unions, and shall enjoy no privileges or subsidies, whether from the government, or from its local autonomous or self-governing institutions.

11. Compulsory demand of collections or dues for the support of ecclesiastical and religious associations, as well as any measures of compulsion or punishment adopted by such associations with respect to their members, are not permitted.

12. No ecclesiastical or religious association has the right to own property. They do not have the rights pertaining to juridical persons.

13. All properties of the existing ecclesiastical and religious associations in Russia are declared to be the property of the people. Buildings and objects of worship shall be delivered, in accordance with the regulations of the local or the central governmental authorities, to respective religious associations for their use, free of charge.[9]

If one reads the decree and takes it at its face value, it is difficult to understand how Marx's thesis that "religion is the opium of the people" and must be wiped out was to be effected. But the application of the law threatened to strangle Orthodoxy. The decree of January 23, 1918, remained on the statute book, but subsequent legislation has distorted it completely.

Soviet laws did not recognize the Church as an organized aggregation of parishes. Any religious organization permitted under the law must have been strictly local in character and completely limited by territorial boundaries. A citizen may be a member of one religious organization, but if he was a member of more than one, he was prosecuted. Each religious organization may have had the use of only one church building and may have performed rites elsewhere only by special permit. Conventions and conferences of more than one organization (i.e., parish) were not permitted to collect money or use church property, vestments, or any articles of worship.

An organized parish that was the only religious unit with legal recognition was deprived of the right to own anything, be it land, buildings, utensils, or vestments. Under the law, a religious unit did not have the right of a judicial person and therefore could not own property or enter into contracts, nor could the unit have the use of an income-bearing property, such as a printing office. All church necessities must have been hired by citizens who contracted with the local soviet. The building was to be given rent free, but the land, which the building occupies, was rented and heavily taxed. Obligatory insurance, local fees, and dues were all added to the burden of those private citizens who contracted for the church building. The number of citizens had to be at least twenty, and they must have assumed personal responsibility for all that would happen within the building as well as maintaining the upkeep and repairs. If any of the twenty were arrested for any reason, or if any law was violated, the church was withdrawn from the religious association. Even donations to the church were restricted heavily by government laws.[10]

Government control over church life was ensured not only by annual reports, but the slightest change in personnel of the church membership, or the executives, had to be reported within seven days. With the changing of laws between 1917 and 1929, any parish was forced to register (a costly act) several times, each time having to fill out endless questionnaires on the history of the parish and each member in it. Local soviets could examine the activities, records, and books of a religious organization at any time. Registration of parishes could be refused by the local soviet with no reason given, and there were no higher courts of appeal.

The limits set on the activities of religious organizations were perhaps the most oppressive of all the laws. A bare performance of religious ceremonies was permitted. All charity work, self-education, teaching of religious doctrine to members and their children, and material assistance to members were strictly forbidden. Even religious ceremonies were not permitted in government, public, or cooperative or private institutions or enterprises. Tolling of the bells was forbidden in all large cities by city ordinance. Funerals could be stopped by civic authorities and often were, on the pretext that they disturbed normal street traffic. The final obstruction came when the government changed the working schedule to a five-day or six-day working week, and the rest days seldom coincided with Sundays. Failure to work on Sundays was reason for dismissal.[11]

In 1923, the decree of January 1918, stating that "citizens may give and receive religious instructions privately,"[12] became void. The number of three children was set for private group instruction and anything over that was punishable by law. By 1929, even this was outlawed, and only parental instruction to one's own children was legal. By law, special theological courses could be offered, but this was so dangerous that only the hardiest souls dared attend the dozen or so courses opened throughout Russia.

These decrees began in December and spread over into January of the new year, precisely at the time that the council was not in session because of the Christmas recess.[13] Patriarch Tikhon, acting alone, issued a solemn proclamation in which the famous anathema was proclaimed.

The humble Tikhon,
by the grace of God patriarch of Moscow and All Russia,
to the beloved in the Lord hierarchs, clergy, and all faithful
members of the Russian Orthodox Church.

"The Lord will deliver us from this present evil world."
(Gal. 1:4)

The Holy Orthodox Church of Christ is at present passing through difficult times in the Russian land; the open and secret foes of the truth of Christ began persecuting that truth, and are striving to destroy the work of Christ by sowing everywhere in place of Christian love the seeds of malice, hatred, and fratricidal warfare.

The commands of Christ regarding the love of neighbors are forgotten and trampled upon; reports reach us daily concerning the astounding and beastly murders of wholly innocent people, and even of the sick upon their sick-beds, who are guilty only of having honestly fulfilled their duty to the Fatherland, and of having spent all their strength in their service for the good of the people. This happens not only under cover of the nocturnal darkness but openly in daylight, with hitherto unheard of audacity and merciless cruelty, without any sort of trial and in defiance of every law and legal principle, and it happens in our days almost in all the cities and villages of our fatherland, as well as in our capital, and outlying regions (Petrograd, Moscow, Irkutsk, Sevastopol, and others).

All this fills our heart with a deep and bitter sorrow and obliges us to turn to such outcasts of the human race with stern words of accusation and warning, in accordance with the command of the holy apostle: "Them that sin reprove in the sight of all, that the rest also may be in fear" (1 Tim. 5:20).

Recall yourselves, ye senseless, and cease your bloody deeds. For what you are doing is not only a cruel deed; it is in truth a satanic act, for which you shall suffer the fire of Gehenna in the life to come, beyond the grave, and the terrible curses of posterity in this present, earthly life.

By the authority given us by God, we forbid you to approach the Mysteries of Christ, and anathematize you, if you still bear the name of Christians and still belong to the Orthodox Church, even if merely on account of your baptism.

I adjure all of you who are faithful children of the Orthodox Church of Christ, not to commune with such outcasts of the human race in any matter whatsoever: "Cast out the wicked from among you." (1 Cor. 5:13)

The most cruel persecution has likewise arisen against the holy Church of Christ; the sacraments of grace, sanctifying the birth of man into the world, or blessing the marital union of the Christian family, have been openly pronounced as unnecessary and superfluous; the holy churches are subjected either to destruction by the deadly gunfire directed against them (e.g., the holy cathedrals of the Moscow Kremlin), or to plunder and sacrilegious injury (e.g., the Chapel of the Saviour in Petrograd). The saintly monasteries revered by the people (as St Alexander Nevsky and Pochaev Lavras) are seized by the atheistic masters of the darkness of this world and are declared to be in some manner the property of the people; schools, supported from the resources of the Orthodox Church to train the ministers of the Church and instructors in faith, are turned either into training institutes of infidelity or even directly into nurseries of immorality. Property of monasteries and Orthodox churches is alienated from them under the guise of being property of the people, but without any right and even without any desire to act in accordance with the lawful will of the people.... Finally, the government which is pledged to uphold right and truth in Russia and to guarantee liberty and order everywhere manifests only the most unbridled self-will and crassest violence over all, and especially in dealing with the Holy Orthodox Church.

Where are the limits to such mockery of the Church of Christ? How and wherein may the attacks upon it by its raging enemies be stopped?

We appeal to all of you, believing and faithful children of the Church; rise up in defense of our injured and oppressed holy Mother.

The enemies of the Church seize rule over her property by force of death-dealing weapons; but you, rise to oppose them with the strength of your faith, with your own nation-wide outcry which would stop those senseless people and would show them that they have no right to call themselves protagonists of the people's welfare, initiators of a new life in accordance with the will of the people, for they are directly against the conscience of the people.

And if it should become necessary to suffer on behalf of the cause of Christ, we invite you, beloved children of the Church, to suffer along with us in accordance with the words of the holy apostle: "Who shall separate us from the love of God? Shall tribulation, or anguish, or persecution or famine, or nakedness, or peril, or sword?" (Romans 8:35).

And you, brethren, hierarchs, and clergy, do not lose even an hour in your spiritual task, and with fiery zeal call upon your members to defend the impugned rights of the Orthodox Church; convene religious gatherings; call them to join, voluntarily, not by force, the ranks of spiritual fighters, who will oppose the external violence with the force of their genuine spirituality; we then positively affirm that the enemies of the church of Christ shall be shamed and shall be dispersed by the might of the cross of Christ, for the promise of the divine Cross-bearer is immutable: "I will build My Church and the gates of hell shall not prevail against it" (Matt 16:18).

Tikhon, Patriarch of Moscow and All Russia

January 19, 1918[14]

This proclamation was read at the first meeting of the council, which reconvened after the Christmas recess, and was given full and enthusiastic support. Many speeches were made acclaiming the patriarch's proclamation. An official resolution was adopted by the council, as follows:

> The Sacred Council of the Russian Orthodox Church lovingly welcomes the proclamation of the most holy Patriarch Tikhon, punishing the malicious evildoers and convicting the enemies of the Church of Christ. From the elevation of the patriarchal throne a word of warning has thundered and the spiritual sword is raised against those who are constantly scoffing at the sanctities of the national faith and conscience. The Sacred Council bears testimony that it remains in the fullest unanimity with the father and intercessor of the Russian Church, responds to his challenge, and is ready to suffer in confessing the faith of Christ, its despisers notwithstanding. The Sacred Council calls upon the whole Russian Church with its hierarchs and clergy at the head to rally around the patriarch, that our holy faith may not be reviled.
>
> (Spinka, *The Church and the Russian Revolution,* 122)[15]

A previously appointed committee submitted a plan of procedure to be adopted by church organizations whenever and wherever the attempt to execute the nationalization of ecclesiastical property should take place. The following instructions were issued:

> 1. Not to surrender anything whatsoever voluntarily to the plunderers of the sacred possessions of the Church, but to guard it according to the example of our pious ancestors.
>
> 2. In case of a forcible demand by anyone whatsoever of any part of the ecclesiastical or monastic property, the rector of the church or monastery should refuse, turning upon the violators with appropriate words of exhortation.

3. The plunderers and robbers of ecclesiastical and monastic property whose names are known should be reported to the diocesan superior, in order that in cases especially revolting they may be excommunicated (canon 3 of St Gregory of Neocaesarea).

4. In case a whole village proves to be guilty of sacrilege and acts of disrespect toward sacred things, the diocesan superior shall order all divine services stopped (with the exception of the sacrament of baptism and of the administration to the sick of the Body and Blood of Christ), and the churches closed, until the guilty shall manifest signs of a true penitence which must be accompanied by the restitution to the church or monastery of everything that has been seized.

5. In case of violence done to priests, the same measures as those described in the previous article shall be adopted.

6. Orthodox brotherhoods should be organized without delay in parish churches and monasteries for the protection of ecclesiastical and monastic property.

7. It shall be the duty of the parochial and monastic clergy to exhort the people, in their sermons in the church, to penitence and prayer, giving the explanation of the current events from the Christian point of view.

(Spinka, *The Church and the Russian Revolution*, 122)[16]

The tension was considerably heightened by the publication of the government decree of January 23, 1918, concerning the separation of the church and state and schools and church. On February 28, 1918, the following instructions were issued by the patriarch and the Synod to all churches:

Appeal to the Priests:

1. Priests are invited to be strictly on guard in protecting the Holy Church in the difficult time of persecution, to encourage, strengthen and unite the believers for defense

against attacks on the freedom of the Orthodox faith and to strengthen the prayers for the correction of those who have gone astray.

2. The priests should encourage the good intentions of the believers directed towards the defense of the Church.

Organization of the Laity:

3. Parishioners of all churches that have parishes and all other churches should be organized into unions (societies) whose duty it shall be to defend the sacred things and church property against violation.

4. These unions must have an educational and charitable character as also a name, and can be presided over by a layman or priest; but could not be called either ecclesiastical or religious societies, as all church and religious societies are by virtue of a new decree deprived of all legal rights.

5. In extreme cases these unions can declare themselves the owners of church property, in order to save them from seizure at the hands of the non-Orthodox or even those of another faith. Let the church building and church property remain in the hands of the Orthodox people who believe in God and are devoted to the Church.

On the Monasteries:

6. The abbots, abbesses, and brotherhood of monasteries, hermitages, and representation churches shall organize similar unions (societies) from among local residents and regular pilgrims to the monastery and all who are loyal to the monastery.

On Ecclesiastical Schools:

7. The principals and teachers in church educational institutions shall establish relations with the parents of the students and the employees, creating unions (societies) for the protection of schools from seizure, and guarantee of their future

activity for the benefit of the Church as also the well-being of the Orthodox people.

8. These unions must firmly demand and endeavour by all means to ensure that the situation in the educational institutions shall remain strictly intact pending further orders of the Church authorities.

9. Teachers of religion in the secular educational institutions should by all means in their power extend their influence over the pedagogical councils and parents' councils, so that they may firmly defend the instruction of religion in a given educational institution and cooperate with every good effort of the same for the benefit of religious training and education.

On the Violence Against the Clergy:

10. The removal by force of the priests and clerics from the parish or monks from the monasteries should under no circumstances be permitted. In case of forceful removal, by the parishioners or outside persons, of the clergy from the posts occupied by them, the diocesan authority shall not fill their places but shall demand that those removed be restored to their former posts, as also the re-establishing of their rights. Every dissatisfaction with a priest or with a member of the clergy should be reported to the Church superiors, which alone have the authority, after investigating the matter, to remove pastors and church employees from the parish.

11. If it should be established that the forceful removal was due to the intrigues of any members of the clergy, the guilty person is subject to a trial by his bishop and strict punishment: a priest will be suspended from his duties, and a psaltist shall be deprived of his clerical position.

On the Seizure of the Church Property:

12. Church vessels and other liturgical appurtenances should be protected by all possible means against desecration and

despoilment, and for this reason they should not be removed from church depositories if not necessary; the latter should be constructed in such a manner that they might not be easily opened by robbers.

13. In case of attempted seizure of church vessels, liturgical appurtenances, church registers, and other church property, the same should not be surrendered voluntarily, inasmuch as

(a) church vessels and other liturgical appurtenances are consecrated by church use and the lay people should not even touch them;

(b) church registers are indispensible for church uses, and the secular authorities, if in need of same, should see to the preparation of them themselves;

(c) church property belongs to the Holy Church, while the clergy and all Orthodox people are merely their guardians.

14. In cases of attack by despoilers or robbers of church property, the Orthodox people should be called to the defense of the Church, sound the alarm and send out the runners, etc.

15. Should the seizure nevertheless take place, it is absolutely necessary to make a report thereof, signed by witnesses with an accurate inventory of the articles seized, indication by name of those guilty of the seizure, and forthwith to report thereon to the diocese.[17]

It was suggested to the patriarch that he should designate a substitute (*locum tenens*) in his place in case he should be arrested or otherwise incapacitated for discharging his office. Parochial brotherhoods were organized throughout Russia to protect the Church, and according to instructions issued by the patriarch and council, they were not able to call themselves ecclesiastical organizations so as not to go against the letter of the January law. Detailed instructions were given to these brotherhoods to help them protect church property and rights.

In Moscow, the central organization of the Moscow parochial brotherhoods appointed twenty-four of their members to serve as the patriarch's bodyguard. They served in two shifts of twelve men each and were instructed to accompany the patriarch on all his journeys and attempt to arouse the masses if any danger were to threaten him.

Much has been made of patriarch Tikhon's interference in politics at the time of the Brest-Litovsk peace. In late February and early March, 1918, rumors of the peace negotiations were everywhere. Before any official announcement was made, Patriarch Tikhon, following in the direct line of historical Church tradition, made a plea to all Russians, of which the following excerpt has been preserved.

> Where is the former might of our country? Where are you, her faithful sons? Are you all perished in bloody struggle, all killed on the battlefields or perhaps you have no more weapons in your hands, no more strength in your muscles, no more flaming fire in your heart? For are not the weapons of death thundering in a mutual internecine warfare and in cruel battles, but not with the enemies of your country, but with your brothers in blood and faith is the power of your muscles and flaming ardour of your heart revealed? And from the battlefield and the face of the foreign enemy you flee with your arms in your hands in order to shoot with these weapons each other in a civil war. How can we be saved from perdition? First of all stop your mutual quarrels and the war.[18]

When the actual announcement of the Brest-Litovsk peace was made, Tikhon's words became even stronger, warning the people that to make peace with the enemy and to continue the internecine war would bring God's judgment. Tikhon spoke of the yearning of the Russian people for peace, but was it peace to leave thousands of Russians in servitude to the

Germans only to continue civil war at home? Using a text from
Jeremiah, Tikhon said:

> Characteristic is the epigraph from Jeremiah—The wise men
> have been put to shame, confounded, they have renounced
> the word of God—wherein is their wisdom? They say peace,
> peace, but there is no peace.
>
> In the face of the dreadful judgment of God which has
> been performed on our country let us rally around Christ
> and our Holy Church.

* * *

> The peace according to which the Orthodox Ukraine is
> separated from Russia and the city of Kiev, the mother of cit-
> ies, the cradle of our baptism, the keeper of our relics ceases to
> be a Russian town, the peace that gives over our own people in
> the Russian lands into servitude, such peace will not give the
> people the desired respite, while it will inflict heavy innumer-
> able losses to the country. Meanwhile we are continuing the
> rift that is annihilating our country. The civil war has not only
> not ceased, but is getting fiercer with every day. The famine is
> increasing, I appeal to all of you archpriests, priests, sons and
> daughters in Christ. Hasten with the preaching of repentance,
> with your appeal to stop the internecine destruction and rift,
> your appeal for peace, quiet, work, love, and unification.

He ended his speech with the following:

> We are called by our conscience to raise our voice in these
> frightful days and loudly to proclaim before the whole world
> that the Church cannot bless the shameful peace now con-
> cluded in the name of Russia.

He urged his followers to harken to the command of God:

> which will correct the evil work that has been wrought and will
> return what has been torn away and will collect the scattered.[19]

In the seventeenth century, before the suppression of the patriarchate by Peter the Great, on Great Friday (Good Friday), the patriarch, humbly reenacting our Lord's entrance into Jerusalem, rode an ass from the Cathedral of the Blessed Basil across the mosaic of fluttering doves through the Saviour's Gate and up to the Kremlin. It was Patriarch Tikhon's idea to reestablish this custom, but upon petitioning the government for the right to make such a pilgrimage, he was curtly forbidden entrance by the ancient way. It was not until late on Easter evening that Tikhon finally was given permission to celebrate Easter on the following day in his own Dormition Cathedral. In spite of all the desecration, crowds of the faithful jammed the cathedral to witness the patriarch officiating. For two hours before midnight, the Acts of the Apostles were read amid the white satin drapes and dim candle-lit icons. More and more candles were lit until at midnight, when the sanctuary doors burst open and the whole church was bathed in light, the eyes of the people were dazzled by the splendor. Then in vestments of royal purple, patriarch, bishops, and priests with silver and crystal crosses joyfully exclaimed, "Christ is Risen," and the crowd cried back, "Indeed He is Risen." The Gospels were thundered in different languages from the four corners of the church and amid the glad cries the festival bell from the tower of Ivan the Great and the mighty voice of the archdeacon Konstantin Rozov[20] rose above the din, praising God and glorifying His name.

During the first year of the patriarchate, Tikhon did a great deal of traveling. In May of 1918, he was invited to Petrograd, and this was probably the happiest time he had during those strife-torn years. Although the Moscow commissars said the patriarch was to have only a simple compartment on the railroad, the railroad workmen insisted that he be assigned a whole carriage for his trip and got their way in this matter. The rector of the Kazan Cathedral in St Petersburg, Archpriest Philosoph Ornatsky, later a martyr, and Bishop Artemy of Luga escorted the patriarch to Petrograd. At the Petrograd station, he was met by Metropolitan Veniamin, also later a martyr, and several priests as well as a great crowd of cheering people who had started collecting about three hours before the train was due. From the station, he was driven in an open carriage to St Alexander Nevsky Lavra and stood up during the entire drive of about a mile and a half, blessing the crowds collected along the streets to see him pass. At the Lavra (monastery), vicar bishops Gennady of Narva, Anastassy of Yamburg, and Melchisedek of Ladoga, two hundred priests, and sixty deacons performed a service. It was at this service that the patriarch preached a sermon pleading for martyrdom of the faithful for Christianity and the Orthodox Church. From the Lavra, he was taken to the hostel (podvorye) of the Trinity–St Sergius Lavra on the Fontanka.[21]

Petrograd was going through a famine at the time. During Tikhon's stay, it was impossible to get the necessary white flour for the blessed bread to be used during the church services. There was no money to pay the choir in St Isaac's Cathedral, so more than fifty deacons sang instead. Complete order was maintained at all of the services. A cross procession was performed at the Kazan Cathedral, and the crowd filled up the square and streets for several blocks. After the procession, Tikhon went to visit Fr Philosoph Ornatsky, whose namesday it was, and for hours the crowd stood under the window of the house. The patriarch came out on the balcony many times to bless the people until the darkness of the night made it impossible to see him. Near the end of his visit, the patriarch visited the Cathedral of St John on the Karpovka and performed a panikhida[22] for Fr John of Kronstadt.

In July 1918, the tsar and his family were murdered by the Soviets. In a crowded service in the Kazan Cathedral in Moscow, the patriarch announced that "the killing of the Sovereign without a trial was the very greatest of crimes and … those who do not condemn this crime will be guilty of his blood."[23] Immediately afterward on July 18, the patriarch and the council held a panikhida for the tsar and his family.

Throughout the eight years of the patriarchate, Tikhon again and again tried to rouse the people to an awareness of their sins. He remained focused on one theme: the Russian people had forgotten God. In a speech given at the New Year in 1918, he said:

> The past year has been a year of the building of the Russian Realm. But alas! does it not remind us of the sad experiment of Babylonian building?

Then he quoted Old Testament prophecies and applied them to the dreadful conditions throughout Russia, stating:

> And all this destruction and confusion is because the Russian Realm is now being built without God. Have we heard from the lips of our rulers the holy name of the Lord in our numerous councils, parliaments, committees? No, they rely solely on their own strength.... We have forgotten God! We have been hunting a new happiness, running after deceptive shadows, have got drunk on the wine of freedom.... The Church condemns such building of ours and we warn most decisively that there will be no success until we remember God.[24]

The new Russian realm was constructed by the power of men, and with the belief in a material world, and this was the sin. No crusaders of the Church were marching in Russia. This was his meaning in the Brest-Litovsk speech. On the first of August, the eve of the beginning for the Dormition Fast,[25] which lasts for a fortnight, he again pleaded with the Russian people:

> This terrible and exhausting night still continues in Russia, and no joyous dawn is to be seen in it. Our Fatherland

succumbs to fierce tortures and there is no remedy that can heal it. So where is the cause of this continued illness, that throws some into apathy, others into despair? Question your Orthodox conscience, and in it you will find the answer to the vexing question. It will tell you that the sin that weighs over us is the source of all your ills and misfortunes. Sin has disintegrated our land. Sin has led the Lord to deprive us according to the word of the prophet (Isaiah 3:1-2) of the staff and the rod and all strengthening by bread, of a courageous leader and warrior, of the judge and the prophet and the wise old men. Sin has darkened the reason of our people and so we are groping in darkness, without light and totter like drunkards (Job 12:25). Sin has fanned everywhere the flames of passion, hostility and ire, and brother has risen against brother, the prisons are filled with captives, the earth is soaked in innocent blood, shed by a brotherly hand, is polluted by violence, pillaging, incest, and other infamies. Sin, heavy and unrepented, has summoned Satan from the abyss, and he is now bellowing his lies at the Lord and His Church and is inaugurating an open persecution of the Church.

O who will give our eyes the necessary tears to bewail all the ills that have been begotten by our national sins and lawlessness—the obscuring of the glory and beauty of our Fatherland, the impoverishment of the land and the exhaustion of the spirit—the destruction of towns and villages, the reviling of churches and holy relics, and all that shattering self-annihilation of a great people that made it into a horrible and shameful spectacle for the whole world.

Where art thou, formerly so mighty and sovereign Russian people? Hast thou completely outlived thy strength? As a giant, magnanimous and joyful, thou hast fulfilled thy great appointed path, heralding peace, love, and truth to all. And now thou liest smitten and cut down by thy enemies, burning up in the flames of sin, passion, and internecine hatred. Is it possible that thou wilt not surge up again, spiritually rise again in power and glory? Has the Lord forever deprived thee of the sources of life, has extinguished thy creative power, in order to cut thee down like a barren tree? May this not be so! The mere thought of it makes us shudder. Weep, dear country, bewail the heavy sins of our Fatherland, before it has perished completely. Weep for yourselves and for those who, because of their hardened hearts, have not the grace of tears.[26]

For some months after the publication of the January 1918 decree of the separation of church and state, the chaotic conditions of the time prevented the provisions from being enforced. In July 1918, however, at the fifth All-Russian Congress of the Soviets, the January decree was restated in even more positive terms. On August 24, a subsequent decree stated:

In order to guarantee to the workers an actual freedom of conscience, the church is separated from the government, and the school from the church, and liberty of religious as well as anti-religious propaganda is granted to all citizens ... members of confessions: Old Ritualist, the Roman Catholic of all rites, the Armenian, Gregorian, the Protestant, as well as the Mohammedan, Buddhist, and Lamaic confessions. Moreover, all other religious associations organized for any type of worship as well as such organizations as are composed of members of one particular confession for the purpose of carrying on any benevolent or educational work or similar objects, are all comprised in the decree separating the church from the government, and are not eligible for aid or subsidy, and lose their juridical rights.[27]

Instructions for use of the churches were rephrased and made stricter. Religious education for the young was restricted further, and the responsibilities for those members of the parish who contracted for the church building were increased heavily. A final insult was added when it was decreed that all monuments and tablets within the church, commemorating any glories of the former tsarist regime, must be removed as "insulting the revolutionary sensibilities of the working masses."[28]

On September 7, the council was being more and more sparsely attended and was dissolved because of lack of funds.[29] It was implied that within three years another council would meet, but no actual provision was made. Thus, Patriarch Tikhon was left with the two committees of the new Church administration to struggle against the Soviet government.

It is difficult to give an adequate description of the Soviet persecution between 1917 and 1921. No complete studies have been conducted, and the few figures that have been used are often from particular sections of Russia and cannot be used for Russia as a whole. Until 1921, there does not seem to be any well-organized drive against the Church directed by a government agency. There were many persecutions, killings, and discriminatory laws, but the application and response usually was unplanned. The Cheka would periodically round up all White suspects and, without a trial, have them shot. Usually, the priests would be the first to be arrested in these local purges. Often mobs would be aroused, whether pro- or anti-Soviet, and a trial of lynchings would ensue. Many of the clergy were arrested, and the Soviet papers carried numerous accounts of the trials and sentences of various bishops. Many people received sentences of exile and perhaps, cruelest of all, clergy of all ranks were excluded from school positions and excluded from all cooperative societies, which in some areas meant slow starvation, deprivation of pensions, and general loss of all citizen privileges.[30]

Emhardt,[31] basing his figures on reports in the *Times* (London), claimed that twenty-eight bishops were killed in 1918 and 1919. For the same time period, he estimated that the number of priests who were executed totaled 1,414. These figures are low when compared with other sources. By 1921, Bolshakoff[32] wrote that of the 1,026 monasteries, 637 had been completely liquidated. Since 1918, no theological books had been printed, no church schools were open, and all candle factories had been forbidden to make church candles.

Following the usual pattern leading to persecution, the January decree was put into effect by local authorities. A rebellion would occur and fighting would break out between the people and the authorities. Often a cross procession would be impetus of the trouble with local authorities, who were determined to break up these processions. In Oryol, Kharkov, and Tula, these religious processions were machine-gunned. Martial law was declared after such outbreaks, and either the leaders of the riot, the clergy, or hostages would be summarily executed. The murder of Metropolitan Vladimir of Kiev was a typical incident, unplanned and without reason.

This type of violence in a country torn by civil strife was a daily affair; men returned from the fronts bearing arms and, having been taught how to use them, continued to do so. The government had its hands occupied with the civil war, and although it did not directly order the persecutions, by its declared program it supported them. Because it was believed that the clergy was the center of monarchist support and certainly the "instruments of that bourgeois reaction whose aim is to defend exploitation by stupefying the working class,"[33] the clergy always was given punishment regardless of the reason for the original incident.

All hope of relaxing the rigor of the new Soviet law was dismissed by the restatement of principles at the Fifth Congress of the Soviets. The Soviets had been in power for almost a year, and conditions not only within the Church but also throughout Russia were deteriorating. In November, on the first anniversary of the Soviet revolution, the patriarch wrote the following letter to the Soviet Commissars:

> All who have taken the sword will perish from the sword. This prophesy of the Saviour we turn towards you, present rulers of our Fatherland, who call yourselves "people's" commissars. A whole year you hold the power in your hands and just get ready to celebrate the anniversary of the October revolution, but the blood of our brothers, shed like rivers and spilled through you, clamors unto heaven and forces us to say to you a bitter word.

Here the patriarch contrasts the promise made by the Bolsheviks with the reality of the chaos evident on all sides:

> Not a day passes without the most monstrous libels in your organs of the press against the Church of Christ. You mock at the servants of the Altar, make bishops dig trenches (Bishop Hermogen of Tobolsk), and dispatch priests to do dirty jobs. You have grabbed the possessions of the Church, collected by generations of the faithful, and have not hesitated to violate their bequests; you have closed a series of monasteries and house churches without any pretext or cause. You have obstructed the passage to the Kremlin— the sanctum of the believers. You have destroyed the time-honored form of the church community, the parish, you do away with the brotherhoods and other charitable educational institutions, you meddle in the self-administration of the Orthodox Church. In throwing out of schools the holy images and in forbidding the teaching of faith in schools, you deprive them of the spiritual food necessary to the Orthodox Christians.
>
> What shall I say? I have no time to describe all the evils that have come over our land. Yes, we are living through the terrible times of your rule and for long it will not efface itself

from the peoples' souls, having obscured in them the image of God and having stamped on them the image of the beast.

We know that our exposure will provoke in you only anger and indignation, and that you will seek in it only a pretext for accusing us of resisting the government, but the higher the pillar of your wrath will rise, the surer testimony there will be of the truth of our exposures.

It is not our task to judge of earthly government. Every government, allowed by God, would attract blessing if it were truly a servant of the Lord for the benefit of the subjects and were a deterrent not for good deeds but for bad (Rom. 13, 34). But now to you who use your powers for the persecution of the innocent, we direct our word of warning. Celebrate the anniversary of your rule by freeing the imprisoned, cease the bloodshed, violence, destruction, persecution of the faith, turn not to destroying, but to maintaining order and laws, give the people their well-deserved rest from civil war. Otherwise you will have to answer for all righteous blood shed by you (Luke 11:51), and from the sword you will perish who have taken it (Matt 25:52).[34]

Although both the Holy Synod and the Supreme Ecclesiastical Council were against the sending of the letter, Tikhon went ahead on his own authority. Many copies were made and distributed widely, but the commissars' only answer was to place the patriarch under house arrest on December 2, 1918. It was at this point that Lenin is credited with having said, "We do not want a second Hermogen."[35] The arrest was lifted the following spring at Easter time.

Throughout the fall, winter, and spring of 1918–19, the rate of persecution increased. An incident that occurred in Kimry provides a typical example. Kimry had five churches for 19,000 people. Of these 19,000, 4,000 were members of the labor union; of these 4,000 members, only 2,031 were actually workmen. The rest of the members chiefly were exiles who did unskilled work. The Church of the Transfiguration, which had an unfinished bell tower, was in the main square next to a maternity clinic. The workmen asked the city soviet to confiscate the church and give it to the hospital. The affair went to the All-Russian Executive Committee, and the Praesidium of the Executive Committee sanctioned the request. In the final sermon at the church, the priest begged the people to be patient and submit. The church people guarded the church, however, and when officials came to seize the church, some of the women resisted. Although the priest was not present at the seizure, he was charged with inciting the revolt, condemned, and executed, and the church was closed.[36]

In view of the increasing stability of the regime, the whole tone of the patriarch's speech a year after his fiery letter to the Bolsheviks had changed. The patriarch commented on the increasing number of executions of the clergy and on the charge of covert counterrevolutionary activity. With the following words, he denied all accusations of subversive acts, and the "establishment of any particular form of government is not the work of the Church, but of the people themselves." Again, he reiterated his ever-constant plea for repentance by the people themselves, for only this would save Russia from disorder and destruction and make the Lord change his wrath to mercy. He spoke of clergymen performing molebens in honor of the advancing Whites, but only at the demand of the new authorities or at the expressed wishes of the people. At no time did the clergy instigate the molebens themselves. He publicly warned the clergy against sympathizing with any of the White movements, reminding churchmen that they must stand apart from all politics. The Church had definite rules forbidding all its clergymen from participating in any intervention in the political life of a country, membership in any party, or the use of divine ritual or priestly ministrations as a tool for political demonstrations.

He closed his speech by reminding the clergy of the Apostle's commandment to "keep from those working dissension and strife" and above all avoid making political utterances or supporting any party.

In the winter of 1919–20, the famous trial of Alexander D. Samarin, Professor Nikolay Kuznetsov, and several monks was conducted by the much-feared Soviet prosecutor, Nikolay Krylenko. The trial was held in connection with the opening of the relics of Venerable Sava of Zvenigorod, but it had the wider task of terrorizing the entire body of Orthodox churchmen. During the trial, Krylenko said, "Samarin and Kuznetsov, these are the general staff, the conscious leaders of that ideology against which the proletariat is fighting to the end without mercy. They have to be eliminated. And all similar leaders from the intelligentsia will come to the same end. The case of patriarch Tikhon is in my portfolio."[37] The tribunal classed those on trial as enemies of the people and sentenced them to be shot, but it later changed the sentence to five years in a concentration camp.

On November 7, 1920, the patriarch, in the face of ever-increasing persecution by the government, published Decree No. 362, of which the following is a pertinent excerpt:

In case that a diocese, because of the fluctuations of the frontline or a change in the borders of the realm, etc., should find itself outside of all communication with the higher administration, or if the higher Church administration with its head—the most holy patriarch—for some reason should terminate its administrative activity, the diocesan bishops should immediately establish contact with the bishops of neighbouring dioceses in order to organize the highest organ of ecclesiastical authority for several dioceses, finding themselves in similar conditions (either in the form of a provisional church government or a metropolitan province or in some other way).[38]

In cases of complete disorganization of church life during which time certain parishes would cease to acknowledge the rule of the bishop of the diocese, the bishop was ordered not to give up his rights, but rather to organize parishes or dioceses that would remain faithful, giving them the power to organize services even in private homes and severing all connections with disobedient parishes.

In actual practice, this meant a complete decentralization of the Church, and it was the official decree on which the refugee churches abroad based their self-government (and still do). Bishops became all-powerful in their sees if the lines of communication to the patriarch and the Synod were cut off, and they even had the right to appoint new bishops in their place without notifying the central administration for confirmation of the appointment.

After Tikhon was made patriarch, he took up his abode in the former apartments of the Metropolitan of Moscow, which were in the representation church (podvorye) of the Trinity–St Sergius Lavra. A contingent of twelve men of the Moscow parochial brotherhood were constantly guarding him, although their value was almost nil, for in case of danger, they were supposed to rouse the people by ringing the church bells. By city ordinance, however, it was illegal to ring any church bells, and a soviet guard was placed in every belfry in the city. The night after he had served a memorial service for the death of the tsar, a rumor went around that the patriarch was to be arrested. A deputation from one of the committees of the Synod was sent to warn him and arrived in the middle of the night, saying they had arranged for his escape abroad. He jokingly chided them for waking him, claiming he wanted to sleep, and then said that escape would be playing into the hands of the enemies of the Church. The deputation spent the night with him and were awed by his peace of mind.[39]

The concern of the Synod for the patriarch's life was well founded. On July 12, 1919, an insane woman, named Guseva, jumped into the carriage of Tikhon as he was leaving Christ the Saviour Cathedral, and knifed him. Fortunately, the patriarch was wearing two tunics because of cold weather, so he received only a slight wound about one and one-half inches in length.

Tikhon traveled all over Moscow officiating constantly in whatever church invited him. He always rode in an open coach with a deacon and one driver. Everywhere people bowed to the carriage, and he blessed them all. On one of his trips, the workmen of Yaroslavl' compelled the town commissars not only to entertain the patriarch and eat with him but also to be photographed with him. In Bogorodsk, the workmen took time to build a special pavilion for him when he visited there.

The Moscow podvorye of the Trinity–St Sergius Lavra was a humble but spacious house with its own church. Next to the altar was a small oratory where the patriarch prayed during services on the few occasions when he was not officiating. The house was surrounded by a small garden where the patriarch often walked late at night. A high fence encircled the garden, but neighboring children climbed the fence and, perched on top, would have long conversations with the patriarch. He always had a store of candy and apples to give to them. The back part of the garden had a small orchard, a vegetable garden, and a collapsing Russian bath house. His diet was chiefly black bread, rationed potatoes without butter, and tea. Throughout his life, however, he remained indifferent to food and was most pleased with simple kasha[40] or shchi.[41] Tikhon's habit, both in business and in entertaining, was to stay up late at night talking quietly in small cozy surroundings, so that the simplicity of life imposed by the revolutionary chaos showed the patriarch to his best advantage and endeared him to all who came into contact with the highest member of the Church, who lived in such a humble yet happy fashion.

CHAPTER 4

Attacks from Within and Without

In the spring and summer of 1921, wide areas of the Volga region and parts of the Ukraine were hit by a tremendous drought. The result of this drought was a complete crop failure in this area, which soon was felt in many parts of Russia. Russia already was in poor condition, torn by years of foreign and civil wars with an almost nonexistent transportation system, poor already in food and horses from requisitioning and other causes, filled with resentful peasants who either hid or destroyed their crops to keep them from the hands of the government officials, and suffering a fantastic loss in buildings from the destruction of the wars. As the winter of 1921–1922 approached, millions of destitute people flocked to the cities seeking food and arrived only to die of starvation on alien ground. Typhus soon broke out and cannibalism became a common horror. The few who survived were forced to eat their horses and planting grain, and thus they had nothing to sow in the spring. The famine spread throughout the twenty-three provinces, and of the thirty-seven million people affected, it was estimated that five million people died of starvation or illnesses resulting from starvation.[1] Charitable assistance poured in from a number of foreign organizations, including the American Relief Administration, the Quakers, the pope, the Nansen Committee, and various trade unions, but the disaster grew increasingly worse.

As early as July–August 1921, Patriarch Tikhon issued an appeal for aid that was addressed to Eastern Orthodox patriarchs and heads of autocephalous churches, the pope, the archbishop of Canterbury, and the Episcopal bishop of New York.² In Russia, an All-Russian Church Committee was organized immediately to raise and collect both money and provisions, and did this with the aid of various parochial brotherhoods. The money and provisions were to be distributed through the administrative channels of the Church to relieve the starving. The government, however, quick to detect a situation in which the Church would gain the gratitude of the people, demanded that all of the collections be turned over to the government for redistribution and declared that the All-Russian Church Committee was superfluous. The Church complied with this demand, but when donors learned that the government had taken over the affair, collections by the parochial brotherhoods dropped considerably and the net results were meager.

The continued spread of the famine made the government realize it would do better to let the Church handle things in its own way, and on December 9, 1921, the following decree was published, which modified the existing regulations:

Decision of the Presidium of the All-Russian Central Executive Committee:

Taking into consideration the long list of solicitations from various religious societies asking for permission to make collections for the relief of the starving, the Presidium of the all-Russian Central Executive Committee decided:

1. To permit the ecclesiastical authorities and the various religious societies to make the collections;

2. To direct the Tsentropomgol (the Central Committee for Aid of the Starving) to enter into an agreement with the religious societies about the method of collection of contributions, having in view the wishes of the donors.

M. Kalinin, President of ACEC
A. Enukidze, Secretary of ACEC
Moscow, Kremlin, December 9, 1921³

Late in 1921 an event outside of Russia occurred that aided the Bolsheviks in their fight against both Tikhon and the Church. A council of émigré clergy and laymen was held in the Serbian town of Sremski Karlovtsi under the chairmanship of Metropolitan Antony (Khrapovitsky) of Kiev, who had been the first to be nominated for the office of patriarch by the 1917 council. The council issued political statements about affairs in Russia for which Patriarch Tikhon was made responsible. The council addressed the international Genoa Conference in January 1922 with the following statement:

> If during this conference, or afterwards, the Bolshevik regime in Russia should receive recognition as the legitimate one, there will result Bolshevik uprisings in one country after another. Their success or prevention depends upon the following measures: 1) upon the nonrecognition of Bolsheviks on the part of all governments; 2) upon the terrible havoc wrought by the famine, cold, and epidemic at present devastating Russia, which has been caused by the Bolshevik mismanagement. Peoples of Europe, and of the world, have pity upon this nation, and equip its sons with arms; then they, together with their dear comrades, officers, generals, and soldiers, will be ready to spring up and march into Russia, to rescue it from its enslavement by the robbers!
>
> Antony, Metropolitan of Kiev and Galicia, President of the
> Russian Ecclesiastical Administration Abroad[4]

At once the Soviet newspapers increased their attacks, trying to prove that Tikhon was at the head of a conspiracy involving the émigré churchmen and the Russian Church and accusing him of ignoring the plight of the people. Demands were made for the treasure of the Church, letters were published[5] written by people who peremptorily asked for the church wealth to buy bread, and imaginary parishes wrote requests saying they wished to give their church treasures but were not permitted to do so. The patriarch authorized his representative at Pomgol[6] to issue a statement to the newspapers indicating that church valuables that held no ritual significance could be donated, but those that had ritual significance could not be touched. As the famine grew worse and the newspaper attacks continued, the newspaper *Pravda* on February 11, 1922, reported that the All-Russian Central Executive Committee immediately would collect all valuables and that the Commissariat of Justice had been instructed to prepare the detailed work for this undertaking. The next day, however, the newspaper *Izvestia* denied that this matter had been decided and claimed that it was to be considered at the next session. On February 24, the blow came when *Izvestia* published a brief announcement that the Central Executive Committee had ordered local soviets to remove all valuables from the churches.

During these two weeks, the newspapers were filled with pleas from various groups[7] demanding that all the church valuables be taken at once. On February 19, Patriarch Tikhon by a special proclamation gave his permission and encouragement to all parochial councils and brotherhoods to give up for the starving masses all unconsecrated ornaments and other objects of value found in the churches, except those used for worship. He stated that to give up any consecrated objects would be a breach of canonical rules. The government permitted this proclamation to be printed and distributed among the people. This justification by canonical rules immediately was seized on by the enemies of the Church and called a flimsy excuse that scarcely hid the callous greed of the Church.

The moment for action was decided, and on February 23, President Kalinin on behalf of the All-Russian Executive Council issued the following decree:

> In view of the necessity for quick mobilization of all the resources of the country to serve as a means of struggle with

the famine in the Volga region, and for the sowing of the fields there, the All-Russian Central Executive Committee, supplementing the decree regarding the removal of property for museums, has decreed:

1. To instruct local Soviets to remove from the ecclesiastical property which was delivered for use of groups of believers of all religions upon inventory and contract, within a month from the day of publication of this decree, all valuable objects of gold, silver, and precious stones, the removal of which cannot actually interfere with the interests of the cult itself; and to transfer them to the offices of the People's Commissariat of Finance, with the special designation for the Fund of the Central Commission for Aid of the Starving.

2. In order that this measure may be properly executed each province must organise a commission of responsible representatives of the provincial executive committee, of the provincial commission of aid for the starving, and the provincial financial department, under the presidency of one of the members of the All-Russian Central Executive Committee for the purpose of giving an account of the above-mentioned valuables as well as for their transfer to the organs of the People's Commissariat of Finance, and for the purpose of rendering a special account to the Central Commission of Aid for the Starving.

3. Revision of the contracts as well as the actual removal of the valuables after their inventory must be done in the required presence of the representatives of the group of believers to whose use the property was transferred.

4. The removed property shall constitute a special fund and must be used exclusively for the needs of the starving, in a manner specified in a special instruction prepared by the Central Committee for Aid of the Starving, with the consent of the People's Commissariat of Finance for the accounting, removing, and collecting of the valuables.

5. A report of all the valuables taken from ecclesiastical property, and of their disposition, shall be made periodically in the newspapers by the Central Commission for Aid of the Starving, and at the same time the local papers must give a detailed description of the valuables taken from the local churches, places of prayer, synagogues, etc., with the specification of the name of those churches.

M. Kalinin, President of ACEC

A. Enukidze, Secretary of ACEC[8]

Within two days, official instructions issued by the Commission directed the removal of ecclesiastical valuables and, in general, amplified the decree. On the very day that the instructions were issued, Patriarch Tikhon's answer was made, which proved to be the final retort of the Church in the long drawn-out bitter struggle between 1917 and 1922:

PROCLAMATION OF THE MOST HOLY PATRIARCH TIKHON REGARDING THE AID FOR THE STARVING.

By the grace of God, humble Tikhon, Patriarch of Moscow and All Russia, to all faithful children of the Orthodox Church of Russia.

May the grace of our Lord Jesus Christ be with you.

Among the heavy calamities and trials which befell the world on account of our lawlessness, the greatest and most terrible is the famine which affected wide regions inhabited by many millions of people. As early as August 1921, when rumors about the terrible calamity began to reach our ears, we, regarding it our duty to come to the aid of our suffering spiritual children, addressed a message to the heads of the several Christian communions (to the Orthodox Patriarchs, the Pope of Rome, the Archbishop of Canterbury, and the Bishop of New York), appealing to them, for the sake of Christian love, to make collections of money and provisions for the starving Volga region people.

At the same time, we established the All-Russian Church Committee for Aid to the Starving and money was being collected in all churches as well as among the various groups, to be devoted to the aid of the famine-stricken. But such a Church committee was declared superfluous by the Soviet government, and all sums already collected by it were ordered to be turned over (and were turned over) to the governmental committee.

However, in December, we were requested to collect, through the mediation of the organs of the Church administration (Holy Synod, Supreme Council of the Church, diocesan councils, and the deanery and parochial councils) money and provisions to aid the starving.

Desiring to cooperate with every possible effort to aid the starving people of the Volga region, we found it possible to permit the parochial councils and societies to sacrifice for the needs of the starving the valuable ecclesiastical ornaments and objects which were not used for the divine services, and we announced this to the Orthodox population on February 6/19 of this year by a special proclamation which the government permitted to be printed and distributed among the people.

But there followed violent attacks upon the spiritual leaders of the Church by the governmental newspapers, and then the All-Russian Executive Committee, in a decree dated February 13/26, for the sake of the aid to the starving, ordered even the consecrated vessels and similar objects used in celebration of the divine services to be removed from the churches.

From the point of view of the Church, such an act is sacreligious and we esteem it our sacred duty to make known the view of the Church regarding the act and to inform our faithful children about it.

In view of the extraordinarily disastrous circumstances, we permitted the possibility of sacrificing church objects which were not consecrated and were not used in the divine services. We exhort all faithful children of the Church even now to make such sacrifices, desiring only that they may be the response of a loving heart to the needs of their neighbor, so that they may actually manifest genuine help to our suffering brethren. But we cannot approve the removal of the consecrated objects from our churches even though it were by way of a voluntary surrender, for their use for any other purpose than the divine service is prohibited by the canons of the Universal Church, and is punishable by her as sacrilege: in case of laymen, by excommunication; clergy by deposition from the sacred orders (Apostolic canon 73; canon 10 of the First-Second Council).

Given in Moscow, February 15, 1922.
The humble Tikhon Patriarch of Moscow and All Russia[9]

This statement was not made public but was distributed secretly by churchmen. For a while the government was ignorant of it, until on March 10, *Izvestia* stated that a copy of the statement had been forwarded anonymously. On March 15, *Izvestia* printed an interview with the patriarch in which he declared: "Remembering the words of Christ, if you have two shirts, give your shirt to your neighbor, the Church cannot remain indifferent to those great sufferings which the starving are experiencing." He also declared that he favored donations of nonconsecrated church articles, but he warned that the amount to be received would not be great.

When the actual confiscation of the church's treasures began, there were many uprisings.[10] Official sources state that more than 1,400 uprisings were recorded, despite the ever-increasing arrests, trials, and executions. *Pravda* and *Izvestia* were filled with records of cases,[11] and they were not restricted only to the Orthodox Church. By early spring, trials were being conducted across Russia, but the most sensational of all was the Trial of the Fifty-Four, which began early in May over opposition to the removal of valuables in Moscow churches. According to the account in *Izvestia*,[12] early in March, Archbishop Nikandr (Fenomenov) of Krutitsy called a general meeting of district priests and read Patriarch Tikhon's message of February 18 against the confiscation of consecrated articles. The district priests in turn held parish meetings reading the patriarchal message and motivating the faithful to resist the government officials.

At this moment, Professor Nikolay Kuznetsov, Bishop Antonin (Granovsky), and two priests (Sergey Kalinovsky and Sergey Ledovsky) testified that according to Church law even consecrated articles could be used for purposes of mercy, and the canons that Tikhon had quoted could merely refer to the confiscation of articles for personal use. Archbishop Nikandr was put on the stand and then was followed on May 9 by a surprise witness, Patriarch Tikhon. The patriarch testified with calmness and dignity that he ruled the Church and its property. He said he was doing only his duty by pointing out the canon laws concerning the confiscation of Church property, and he still felt that the government was making a mistake in ordering the confiscation. He stated that clergymen were not bound to obey his orders but that it was his task to issue them. At the end of his testimony, Patriarch Tikhon quietly but firmly declared that as the author of the February edict, he alone was guilty of the charges against the fifty-four and that he alone should bear the penalty.

This was exactly what the prosecution had been waiting for. At once the spotlight of the trial was turned on the patriarch, and newspapers took up the hue and cry. The patriarch was accused of heading a monarchist plot to overthrow the government, he was held responsible for the Karlovtsy Synod's appeal to the Genoa Conference, all uprisings were declared to have been instigated by him, the whole clergy was called the "foulest, blackest foes of the working people and the revolution."[13] The Trial of the Fifty-Four ended with the death penalty for five clergy members and long prison sentences were given to the rest. Most important, the Moscow Tribunal ruled that, from the evidence presented during the trial, a hierarchy composed of Archbishop Nikandr and Patriarch Tikhon had worked out a complete plan of opposition against the removal of consecrated valuables, had distributed the description of this plan, and had produced excessive uprisings. In view of this finding, the Tribunal set about indicting Patriarch Tikhon and Archbishop Nikandr.

Long before the May trial, Patriarch Tikhon's freedom had been curtailed. By the end of February and beginning of March, his absence was noticed and the news of his house arrest traveled swiftly. Great crowds collected outside his apartment every day, and only by his frequent appearances at the window would the people believe that he was still alive. Soon the patriarch was transferred to the Donskoy Monastery, where he was guarded closely; much later, he was placed in one of the Moscow prisons of the State Political Department.

On May 5, the day of the opening of the Moscow Trial of the Fifty-Four, in an attempt to save the lives of the defendants, Patriarch Tikhon with the Synod ruled that the Higher Russian Church Administration Abroad, which had called the Karlovtsy Council, had no legal status, and because its acts were purely political, they had no ecclesiastical significance. The council was declared dissolved, and the Synod was told to collect all evidence to consider whether to put the Karlovtsy Council members on trial and when the Russian Synod could return to a normal state and have its full membership. The patriarch also declared that Metropolitan Evlogy (Georgievsky),[14] who had been raised to a metropolitan by Tikhon on January 30, 1922, alone possessed full jurisdiction over the Russian churches abroad. This proclamation, however, was far less than the Soviet government desired, which was full excommunication of all members of the Karlovtsy Council, and was not viewed as a sign of good will on the part of the patriarch.

In August 1922, Petrograd was the scene of even more sensational trials of the clergy. During the summer, the papers had recorded nine violent instances of opposition in Petrograd by the people to the government officials who attempted to confiscate consecrated items. Bells were rung, crowds gathered, troops were beaten and stoned, and the inevitable killings took place on both sides. Eighty-six people were accused, the most notable being Metropolitan Veniamin (Kazansky) of Petrograd. Much of the testimony that was used to convict Veniamin came from two members of the Petrograd clergy, Vladimir Krasnitsky and Alexander Vvedensky,[15] who had become the ringleaders of a revolutionary movement within the Church. Both of these men had been excommunicated and deprived of their offices by the Metropolitan Veniamin, and they were known as open enemies of the metropolitan. The whole trial was based on a theme of counter-revolution by the Church. The prosecutor P. Krasikov dwelt on the record of the Church as a perpetual opponent of the Soviet government and supporter of the White movement, and the leader of the Church, Patriarch Tikhon, was described as being directly responsible for the Karlovtsy Council. The verdict finally was reached on July 6, 1922, and ten of the accused were sentenced to be shot whereas the rest drew jail sentences, the length of which depended on their alleged guilt.

Complete figures of the confiscations were never issued, but as of October 1, 1922, Pomgol reported that the following had been received by the local offices of the Commissariat of Finance: 1,217 pounds avoir of gold valued at 600,000 gold rubles; 863,913 pounds of silver valued at 18,500,000 gold rubles; and 4,268 pounds of other metals valued at 211,563 gold rubles. The total equaled 19,300,000 gold rubles.[16]

In December, *Izvestia* stated that the financial results of the confiscations were completely unsatisfactory as a result of undue mildness on the part of the local authorities and concealment or theft by the churchmen. The statistics on those who were imprisoned and killed as a result of this attack by the government on church valuables are equally incomplete. Brikhnichev, a Soviet writer, has estimated these figures based on sentences passed by fifty-five tribunals, but they are far from complete. Of 738 persons tried, 149 were acquitted, 33 were shot, 75 were put on probation, and the rest received prison terms; of the condemned, 181 were clergy and 408 were laymen.[17]

In May 1922, a revolution within the Orthodox Church came closer to destroying the Church in Russia than any decree issued by the Bolsheviks. The roots of the revolution lay far back in the early history of the Church, but more traceable evidence of the crisis can be seen in the revolution of 1905. At the time of the revolution of 1905, a group of revolutionary clergy was formed in St Petersburg and supported by that everlasting agitator Bishop Antonin.[18] This same group can be seen in the council of 1917 under the name of the All-Russian Union of Democratic Clergy led by the priests Alexander Vvedensky, Alexander Boyarsky, John Egorov, Dmitry Popov, and others. The liberal professor Boris Titlinov,[19] aided by Vvedensky and his group, tried to organize an underground movement within the Church but nothing came of these efforts.

Easily led people existed among the clergy as everywhere, however, and the absence of all restraint and the corresponding lowering of the general moral level of society made an imprint on certain churches. Slowly and quietly, certain innovations began to creep into the services, and a so-called modernization of the church ritual was preached by the revolutionary spirits until the changes became so obvious that the patriarch's attention was directed toward them. On November 17, 1921, Tikhon sent out a message, refusing to bless such innovations and requesting that they be stopped immediately. He promised that the whole question of permitted innovations would be examined and dealt with by the next council.[20]

Another tendency of the so-called progressives among the churchmen was to copy the propaganda of the revolution and attempt to impose on the Church problems of a social and political character of life on this earth, while ignoring the Church's real problems of man's soul and its relation to the next world. Questions of crime, poverty, and others not of a spiritual nature confused the faithful who began to look to the Church for material consolation, rather than spiritual aid. The difficulty of this position was the lack of a real dividing line between the two worlds, and the Church progressives eagerly obliterated any faint divisions that existed between material and spiritual solace.

One of the oldest problems of the Church was the ever-present rivalry between the Black or monastic clergy and the White or married clergy. Because all bishops had to be monks, the administration of the Church was in the hands of the Black clergy, and this was deeply resented by certain parish priests. Part of the Church revolution actually was an attempted Protestant reform of the administrative level.

Another strand to be found in the revolutionary skein of threads was the attempted bridge built on air between Christianity and Communism. Add the men who were swayed by the baser passions of power, greed, vanity, and revenge to these influencing factors, and one can understand the revolutionary movement within the Church.

With the ever-increasing attack of the government over the confiscation of the church valuables to aid the famine fund and the sensational Moscow Trial of the Fifty-Four, the revolutionary group felt that now was the time to strike. On March 25, 1922, the following letter was printed in *Krasnaya Gazeta* and reprinted in *Izvestia* on March 29:

PROCLAMATION OF A GROUP OF PRIESTS
    The events of the last few weeks have settled beyond all doubt the actuality of two divergent views in church circles

regarding the aid to the starving. On the one hand, there are churchmen, who, out of principle (on account of one or another theological or non-theological consideration), do not desire to sacrifice any treasures for the purpose of aiding the starving. On the other hand, there is a multitude of other church people who are ready, in order to save the dying, to make every kind of sacrifice, including the conversion of the church treasures into bread to feed the hungering Christ (for hungering Christ see Matt 25:31–46).

Some members of the hierarchy of the Russian Church have already authoritatively spoken about the necessity of coming to the aid of the starving, with all the apostolic zeal, even with the church treasures: for instance Archbishop Evdokim, Archbishop Seraphim, Archbishop Mitrophan, and a number of other hierarchs, as well as many archpriests and priests.

Such wicked unprovocative talk (against aiding the starving) convicts the individuals of the clerical order who think in such manner, of being traitors and masked enemies of the Church. God and the public conscience will be their judges.

However, that openly unchristian feeling of malice, heartlessness, and slander, the confusing of the church with politics, and so forth, obliges us to make the following declaration:

It is no secret for those acquainted with the situation that a certain element in the Church belongs to it not with their heart or soul, but with their body only.

The faith of Christ does not permeate their whole being, does not constrain them to act and to live in accordance with itself.

That is thought to be the case especially among that number of ecclesiastics among whom the feeling of malice exists, and hence plainly witnesses to the absence of Christ (John 18:35).

One's heart is pained by it, and the soul weeps.

Brethren and sisters in the Lord!

People are dying! Old men are dying, children are dying. Millions are doomed to perish. Have not your hearts been moved yet?

If Christ be with us, where then is his love toward all—the near and the distant, the friends and the enemies? Where is the love which, according to God's word, is higher than the law? Where is the love which is ready to overcome all obstacles in order to render aid? For indeed it was such love which the Lord taught us. Is it impossible to be comprehended?

The heartlessness, the human calculation of some which was manifested so sadly in connection with the famine, constrain us to speak plainly; we, Christians, must conform our lives to the commands of Christ.

In particular, regarding the question of church treasures and the possibility of their use for famine relief, we assume that it is our moral and Christian duty to make the sacrifice. Indeed, theoretically, that is what even Patriarch Tikhon and Metropolitan Veniamin and other hierarchs permitted us to do.

The believers will willingly come to the aid of the government if no violence be used (regarding which official authorities assure us). The believers are willing to surrender, if need be, even the sacred vessels, if the government will permit the Church itself to feed the starving, even though it be done under a strict governmental supervision; the authorities have expressed themselves to the effect that such an arrangement would be possible.

Thus we shall be ready for sacrifices, and resolutely separate ourselves from those who calling themselves Christians, in the matter under consideration look upon it differently and in such wise follow and invite others to the path of indifference toward those who are dying of starvation, and even to the culpable, Christian-forbidden path of violence in defence of the church treasures.

Churchmen! An unfortunate misunderstanding of that question has separated us! We must, with mutual love, with mutual respect, and burning with love for those of our brethren who are perishing of starvation, help them all, even to the surrender of our lives. That is what Christ expects of us!

Archpriests: John Albinsky, Alexander Boyarsky, Alexander Vvedensky, Vladimir Voskresensky, Eugene Zapolsky, Michael Popov, Paul Raevsky

Priests: Eugene Belkov, Michael Gremyachevsky, Vladimir Krasnitsky, Nicholas Syrensky
Deacon Timothy Skobelev[21]

On March 30, Bishop Antonin, one of the leaders of the insurgent group and a state witness in the Trial of the Fifty-Four, was appointed to Pomgol as a government representative to supervise the stripping of the churches. *Izvestia* printed a letter from Antonin to the patriarch in which Antonin said that Kalinin had appointed him personally because "of the desire of the government to give to the church people through me a possibility of supervision of the disposition of the treasures, their exchange for currency, and the purchasing of bread for the starving with the money thus realized."[22] Given the patriarch's decree, this letter could not have been more provocative.

On May 12, the newspaper *The Living Church,* put out by the reformers, as they styled themselves, printed an article by Vladimir Krasnitsky demanding a change in the higher personnel of the church. Vvedensky and Antonin also wrote attacks on the Church's stand and on the patriarch personally. The most important part of the new publication, however, was a proclamation to "the believing sons of the Orthodox Church of Russia," which was a direct challenge to the patriarch, showed the true position of each group, and clearly defined those who were designated to lead the revolutionary group for the next few years.

Brethren and sisters in Christ!

In the course of the last few years, in accordance with the will of God, without which nothing in the world comes to pass, the government of workers and peasants came into power in Russia. It took upon itself the task of liquidating the heavy consequences of the World War, a struggle with the famine, epidemics, and the remaining disorders of the governmental life.

The Church in the meantime, remained aloof from the great struggle for truth and the wellbeing of humanity.

The heads of the Church were on the side of the enemies of the people.

This became manifest, insofar as every current incident was accompanied by a counter-revolutionary uprising within the Church. Such things happened more than once. At the present time, similar sad occurrences have taken place before our own eyes, in the matter of converting the church treasures into bread for the perishing brother, but it was converted into a conspiracy against the government.

It resulted in bloodshed. Blood was shed that the hungering Christ might not be aided.

By the refusal to help the starving, churchmen were attempting to bring about the overthrow of the government. The proclamation of Patriarch Tikhon became the standard around which rallied the counter-revolutionaries, outwardly disguised in ecclesiastical garb.

But the wider masses of the people and the majority of the rank and file of the clergy did not heed their call. The popular conscience condemned those guilty of shedding blood, and the death of those who succumbed to the famine falls with a heavy reproach upon those who wished to exploit the national calamity for their own political ends.

We, the undersigned clergy of the Orthodox Church, representing the opinions of wide ecclesiastical circles, condemn the actions of those hierarchs and those pastors who are guilty of organizing opposition to the governmental authorities in the matter of aiding the starving and in other undertakings for the good of the workers.

The Church by its very essence should represent a society of love and truth and not a political organization, or a counter-revolutionary party.

We consider it necessary that a local Sobor be called without delay for a trial of those who are guilty of the ruin of the Church, as well as to order the ecclesiastical government, and to establish normal relations with the Soviet authorities. The civil war which is carried on by the supreme administration against the government must be stopped.

Every faithful and loving son of the Church will doubtless approve our petition with which we appealed to the government authorities asking to grant us the permission to call a local Sobor speedily for the purpose of ordering the Church and pacifying the national life.

Bishop Antonin

Representatives of the progressive clergy of Petrograd:
Priest Vladimir Krasnitsky, Archpriest Alexander Vvedensky,
Priest Eugene Belkov, Psaltist Stephan Stadnik[23]

Now that the position of the reformers had been made clear to the public, it had to be followed up by action. On the same day that this proclamation was published, a delegation consisting of the archpriest Vvedensky, the priest Belkov, and the psaltist Stadnik interviewed the patriarch, who was already under house arrest. On arriving in Moscow, they were joined by the two priests Krasnitsky and Kalinovsky and went straight to the Trinity–St Sergius podvorye. Tikhon had not seen the belligerent letter that was just being published. Krasnitsky acted as spokesman for the group; using the outcome of the trial three days before as the basis, in which Tikhon had been called as a witness and eleven death sentences[24] had been given, he charged the patriarch with counterrevolutionary activities.

He listed Tikhon's anathema of January 19, 1918, as counterrevolutionary, as well as the patriarchal instructions of
February 15, 1918, that had instructed priests to secrete church
property so that it could not be found by government officials
and ordered the organizing of parochial brotherhoods for the
defense of church property. He held Tikhon responsible for
the 1,414 bloody encounters that, he claimed, had resulted
from these orders. He held it as a counterrevolutionary action
to have sent the patriarchal blessing and blessed bread to
the imprisoned tsar at Yekaterinburg, to have ordained and
appointed people who were known to be promonarchist, and
to have converted the Church into a political organization
that under the screen of spiritual concerns was attempting to
overthrow the Soviet regime. In view of these charges and the
present anarchy of Church affairs, the delegation demanded
an immediate calling of a national council, the inauguration of
new Church policies, and the patriarch's complete abdication
of authority until the next council would pass on the pending
questions.

Vvedensky[25] later wrote a detailed description of the interview, and according to him, the patriarch finally said, "I have
not sought the patriarchal office, and it weighs me down like
a cross. I shall retire from the administration of the Church,
and shall transfer my authority to the eldest of the hierarchs."
He then sat down and wrote a letter to President Kalinin of
the All-Russian Central Executive Committee speaking of
his intention to transfer his patriarchal authority to another
hierarch and then dispatched a message to Metropolitan
Agathangel of Yaroslavl' in which he appointed him as the
patriarchal *locum tenens* and asked him to come to Moscow
to take over his new duties. These two letters officially closed
the patriarchal chancery for the time being.

The appointment of Metropolitan Agathangel was apparently a setback to the delegation,[26] for during the interview
they had demanded that Bishop Antonin be appointed as the

patriarch's successor. Moreover, to force this request, Vvedensky said that the eleven churchmen condemned to be shot might be pardoned if the patriarch consented to this demand. The patriarch refused to consent, and speaking of the adverse Soviet attitude to Metropolitan Veniamin, he selected Metropolitan Agathangel as his successor.

On May 18, a second interview took place between the delegation and the patriarch at the Trinity–St Sergius podvorye. The room in which the patriarch received the plotters was a large mid-Victorian chamber, rather shabbily furnished with ancient carved and upholstered sofa and chairs and two tables covered with old fashioned table covers. The walls were adorned with a few Italian-style oil paintings representing former patriarchs.[27] From the windows, one could see into the garden that in 1926 was turned into an amusement place by one of the Communist organizations. The conference lasted one and one-half hours, during which time the following document was impudently presented to the patriarch:

To the Most Holy Patriarch Tikhon;

In view of the removal of Your Holiness from the administration of the Church until the time of the calling of the Council, and of your transfer of authority to one of the elder hierarchs, the Church remains at present, as a matter of fact, without any kind of administration.

That circumstance shows itself extraordinarily detrimental to the course of general church life, and especially in Moscow, exciting thereby a great disturbance of minds.

We, the undersigned, have petitioned the governmental authorities for permission to open the chancery of your holiness and start its functioning.

By the present letter we finally ask for Your Holiness's blessing upon it, in order that the harmful cessation in the administration of church affairs be terminated.

Your Deputy, then, upon his arrival, will immediately enter upon the discharge of his duties.

For these labours in the chancery, until such a time as the final formation of the administration under the headship of your deputy be accomplished, we temporarily engage bishops now at liberty in Moscow.

The unworthy servants of Your Holiness,

Archpriest Alexander Vvedensky

Priest Eugene Belkov

Priest Sergius Kalinovsky[28]

Along with the document, the delegation expressly stated that the arrangement was only temporary until the arrival of the *locum tenens*, at which time the delegation would instantly retire from their duties. To guarantee that the chancery would be run correctly and Church business would be reestablished along orderly lines, out of its present chaos, they promised to include among their numbers whatever bishops were still in Moscow at liberty. The one bishop immediately included was, of course, Bishop Antonin. In vain, the patriarch tried to foresee what possible results could come from his consent, and then, swayed by the chaos of a closed chancery, and believing the Moscow bishops could control the reformers, he wrote the following at the top of the same document:

May 5 (o.s.), 1922. The persons named below are ordered to take over and transmit the synodal business to the Most Reverend Metropolitan Agathangel, upon his arrival in Moscow, with the assistance of Secretary Numerov; (administration of) the Moscow diocese (to be entrusted) to the Most Reverend Innocent, bishop of Klin, and before his arrival to the Most Reverend Leonid, bishop of Vernyi, with the assistance of the departmental chief Nevsky. For the hastening of my departure and the lodging in the patriarchal residence of the Most Reverend Agathangel, I beg that Archimandrite Anempodist (Alekseev) be given leave.

Patriarch Tikhon[29]

The following day, Tikhon was removed from the Trinity–St Sergius podvorye to the Donskoy Monastery on the outskirts of Moscow, which became his headquarters until he died. On May 20, *Izvestia* reported that the progressive group with permission from the patriarch had moved into the former patriarchal residence and were operating the chancery. Then, without patriarchal permission, they organized themselves into the Provisional Higher Ecclesiastical Administration headed by Bishop Antonin and Bishop Leonid, the only one of the number mentioned by patriarch Tikhon in his instructions, appointing temporary administrators of the Moscow diocese. Other members of the administration included Vvedensky, Krasnitsky, Kalinovsky, Belkov, Albinsky, Polikarpov, and Meshchersky. An announcement of a new council to be called soon was made at once.

In the meantime, Patriarch Tikhon's *locum tenens*, Metropolitan Agathangel, was refused the necessary permission to leave Yaroslavl'. Emhardt[30] claimed he had positive proof that he was approached by a member of the Higher Church Administration and asked to join the revolutionary movement but that he categorically refused. In June, he issued a message to the faithful, which was distributed secretly, calling upon all the Orthodox not to recognize the new Church administration, but rather to remain faithful to the patriarch. Following Decree No. 362 of 1920, the bishops were to rule their diocese in autonomous fashion until the true Church authorities were restored. The said proclamation of Agathangel was posted in many of the Moscow churches, and a few days later *Pravda* reported that the "Black Hundredite and counter-revolutionary" Metropolitan Agathangel, who was posting proclamations counseling nonrecognition of the new liberal movement within the Church, was under house arrest. Soon after his arrest, he was exiled to Narym in Siberia, one of the least healthy spots in Russia. Bishop Innocent, also named by Tikhon to conduct the Church administration, was unable to get permission to leave his diocese for Moscow.

On May 29, 1922, a constituent conference of the Living Church was held in Moscow attended by 146 delegates. Only thirty-six people voted to adopt the platform and in a sense became the founding fathers of the new organization. The dogmatic reforms were chiefly in a return to primitive Christianity. God was to be taught through the humanity of Christ. The universe was declared to be evolved by the might of God by means of natural processes. The Church was to help realize the divine truth on earth.

Ethically, the monastic teaching of salvation through renunciation of the world was rejected, and instead the faithful performance of ordinary duties and labors was declared to be the best method of salvation. The social revolution was praised as defending the rights of the former exploited working class. Liturgical forms were to be reappraised and any tsarist innovations were to be dropped. Liberty of liturgical creativity was to be encouraged at all times. Canonical reform was to be immediately undertaken, again with the purpose of dropping such rules and canons as dated from tsarist times. Priests were to be elected by the congregation, laymen given much more power in the Church. The episcopate were now to be chosen from among both the Black and White clergy, but the authority of the old episcopate was to be shared by laymen, clergy, and bishops equally.

As for relations with the state, the Living Church declared itself in every way to be supporting the revolution, condemning the strained relations of Tikhon to the government, and willing to accept the complete separation of church and state according to Soviet law.[31]

A third public meeting was held at the end of June, and a formal Church party organization was set up. A central administrative and executive committee was elected with Vladimir Krasnitsky at the head. When the platform was announced to the public, a riot took place, with the audience, chiefly composed of women, violently threatening and protesting the platform.

Between August 6 and 16, 1922, the Living Church held an All-Russian Conference in the Cathedral of Christ the Saviour in Moscow. This conference was a small, highly selective gathering open only to ecclesiastics. A hundred laymen appeared, however, and after ascertaining that they were favorable to the Living Church, Krasnitsky permitted them to attend. Twenty-four dioceses were represented, and 190 delegates attended. The hostility of most of the delegates to the Black clergy soon showed itself in a resolution that closed all city monasteries and convents, for "monks by their very profession have no place in the turmoil of life," and country monasteries were to become centers of socially useful work, such as clinics.[32] On the same day, the following resolution was passed:

1. That the Living Church group should demand at the next sobor that Patriarch Tikhon be deposed from the sacred orders, because he bears the chief guilt for the present disorganization of the Church.

2. That the Supreme Ecclesiastical Administration be petitioned to order an immediate cessation of the mention of his name in the liturgical services in all parishes of the Russian Orthodox Church, as of one who no longer holds office.[33]

A report then was presented on the Church views of the one-hundred and forty-three active bishops. Thirty-seven were counted as pro–Living Church, thirty-six were definitely opposed, and the rest were undeclared. The conference decided on immediate removal of the thirty-six anti–Living

Church and said that the undecided bishops must immediately
state their position. A few days later, it was announced at the
conference that twenty-four more bishops had been retired
in addition to the thirty-six opposing ones; this made a total
of sixty forcibly retired bishops. In many cases the GPU
(political police)[34] very willingly aided the Living Church by
arresting stubborn ecclesiastics and sending them into exile
on the usual charge of counterrevolution. Before the adjourn-
ment an address to the people was adapted that recounted
the charges against the patriarch and described the policies of
the new administration. The following excerpts refer to the
charges against Tikhon:

> Five years of civil war, heavy sacrifices borne by our fami-
> lies, enormous economic upheaval, millions of the sons of
> Russia killed and wounded in that war—all these are the
> fruits of the criminal treason against the Russian working
> people which our Orthodox hierarchs committed by siding
> with the national enemies. In the armies of Kolchak, Denikin,
> Wrangel, Yudenich, and the other robbers who were cruelly
> plundering the Russian land and who, one after another,
> escaped abroad with the plundered property of the Russian
> people, they, our hierarchs, occupied honorary places, vio-
> lently took part in the plundering, all the while excusing and
> blessing the atrocious lawlessness. To crown it all, last win-
> ter they gathered themselves at Karlovtsy, together with the
> runaway owners and prominent officials of the former tsarist
> regime, and engaged in instigation of popular uprisings and
> a new civil war under the guise of guarding church treasures
> which were consigned to aid those who were dying of star-
> vation. Our supreme pastors with Patriarch Tikhon at their
> head, in order to preserve in our Orthodox churches gold,
> silver, and precious objects, falsely expounded the canons,
> caused disturbance among the faithful, and instigated com-
> motion, local revolts, and bloodshed.[35]

The reformist group itself had no real unity, however, and this became clear after the August conference. Krasnitsky was the leader of the group, which was able to control the conference and succeeded in putting over his entire program, but a more moderate party headed by Bishop Antonin on August 20 split off under the name of the "Union for the Regeneration of the Church." They were concerned chiefly with the evils of clericalism and sacerdotalism, which they felt had crept into the Church since the time of Christ. Most interesting in their program was that a bishop must be unmarried, although he could be from the White or Black clergy. Archpriest Vvedensky, one of the first revolutionaries, also split off and formed a group called the "Union of the Communities of the Ancient Apostolic Church," which was concerned with dogma reform.

At once the struggle was taken to the parish level and here the fate of the Living Church ultimately was decided.[36] On August 22, it was decreed that all parishes must reregister and those that proved hostile to the Living Church were to be refused a building. Laymen contracting for the church had to declare publicly for the reformers or they were refused a contract, and since priests were to be elected by the congregation and the congregation had to be pro–Living Church, the priest also must be reformist. Priests along with the bishops lost their jobs and usually ended up in concentration camps.

The patriarchal church, in defense, organized new dioceses following Decree No. 362,[37] but since they were unable to register them, the new dioceses were illegal in the eyes of the Soviet law and therefore completely without status. Strangest of all, because only parish organizations had any legal existence within the framework of Soviet law, the actual Living Church organization set up in the August conference[38] was illegal, and yet it was this organization that claimed to rule the Orthodox Church.

On February 1, 1923, a council was to be held by the Living Church that they designated as the Second All-Russian

Council, but the purging of those ecclesiastics faithful to Tikhon had not gone far enough to ensure that the Living Church would have a majority, so the council was canceled until April 29. Means were established to limit carefully the membership of this council. Only those believers who were enrolled with their parish priest and had obtained a certificate of good standing from him could vote for representatives. Also any persons tried and convicted during the reform period were forbidden to vote. This included all the Tikhonite clergy who had been ousted by the Higher Church Administration. To add to these precautions, the Living Church had a number of ex-officio or invited members, including the Higher Church Administration, the administrations of the Church in Ukraine and Siberia, and the fifty-six diocesan commissioners of the Higher Church Administration. A final check was made by requiring a detailed questionnaire to be filled out by each delegate regarding his views on the activity of the patriarch, views on the Soviet government, views on the proposal to depose the patriarch, former political activity, and views on the patriarch's anathema.

When the council finally met on April 29, 476 delegates were present. The Living Church had the largest contingent with 250 delegates, Vvedensky's Ancient Apostolic Church had 110 delegates, and Bishop Antonin's Union for the Regeneration of the Church had 25 delegates. Forty-five delegates were adherents of the patriarch, having somehow gotten past all the screening, and the remaining forty-six attended as guests with no right to vote.

On the first day, official welcoming speeches were made in the Cathedral of Christ the Saviour in Moscow, a liturgy was served and prayers were said for the government. Praise followed praise: for the separation of church and state decree, the revolution, and the overthrow of capitalism, and the comedy was crowned when a "many years"[39] was sung to the new government. On the second day, Lenin himself was sent a complimentary address from the council, which according to the records was adopted unanimously. On May 3, while the patriarch was still imprisoned in the monastery, the council without trial and without any counsel for the defense passed the following resolution:

> After adjudicating the activity of Patriarch Tikhon, the episcopal council came to the unanimous decision that Patriarch Tikhon is subject, before the conscience of the believers, to the heaviest penalty; to the punishment of deprivation of his clerical orders and of his patriarchal office, because he had directed all his powers of moral and ecclesiastical authority toward the overthrowing of the existing civil and social order of our life, and thus brought into jeopardy the very existence of the Church.[40]

Fifty-four hierarchs signed it, but because sixty-six hierarchs attended, twelve bishops (unnamed) must have refused.[41] Vvedensky then delivered a tirade lasting two and one-half hours against the patriarch, of which the following excerpt was put into a resolution:

> After the meeting of the Council, Patriarch Tikhon continued this counter-revolutionary activity. He became the leader and standard bearer of all opponents of the Soviet government. He drove the Church into the counter-revolutionary struggle.
>
> The Sacred Council of the Orthodox Church of 1923 condemns the counter-revolutionary struggle and its methods, which are the methods of man-hatred. Especially does the Council of 1923 deplore the anathematization of the Soviet government and of all who recognize it. The Council declares this anathematization to have no force.
>
> The Council of 1923 condemns all those who have followed this path and persuaded others to follow them.

And this applies, first of all, to the responsible leader of our church life, Patriarch Tikhon. Whereas Patriarch Tikhon served the counter-revolution instead of sincerely serving Christ, and since he is the person who was supposed to direct properly all ecclesiastical life, but as on the contrary he led astray the broad masses of the Church, the Council regards Tikhon as an apostate from the original commands of Christ and a traitor to the Church. On the basis of the canons of the Church, it hereby declares him to be deposed from the sacred orders and monasticism and relegated to his original status of a layman.

Hereafter Patriarch Tikhon is layman Vasily Bellavin.

* * *

Condemning the former Patriarch Tikhon as a leader of counterrevolution and not the Church, the Council holds that the very restoration of the patriarchate was a definitely political counter-revolutionary act. The ancient Church knew no patriarch and was governed conciliarly; hence the Sacred Council hereby abolishes the restored patriarchate: hereafter the Church shall be governed by the Council.[42]

Having reduced the title of patriarch to citizen Bellavin, apostate and traitor, the council then confirmed the election of the White clergy to bishoprics, permitted priests to remarry, and in a final grand gesture adopted the Gregorian calendar as of June 12, 1923. On May 4, a special delegation of the council visited Tikhon, who was confined in the Donskoy Monastery. He was informed of the decision of the council and asked to sign the formal notification. With complete calmness, he wrote his name, one word being quietly added: "illegal."

CHAPTER 5

The Release

For more than a year, Patriarch Tikhon had been imprisoned, supposedly waiting for a trial on charges that had
been grown out of the Moscow Trial of the Fifty-Four and
the Petrograd trials of Metropolitan Veniamin and those connected with him. On April 16, 1923, the Trial Collegium of the
Supreme Court announced that it would begin to hear the case
of the former patriarch, Archbishop Nikandr; Petr Guryev,
head of the Synodal chancery; and Metropolitan Arseny (Stad-
nitsky) of Novgorod. The charges against Tikhon were that he
had had "dealings with foreign powers, counter-revolutionary
work directed toward overthrowing the Soviet order, opposition to decrees of the authorities, and using religious beliefs
and prejudices for creating a disobedient and rebellious attitude among the masses."[1] Furthermore, the patriarch was
accused of always having opposed the Soviet regime, having
supported the Whites, and having dealings with the Karlovtsy
Synod. He was made personally responsible for the violence of
the people's opposition to the government officials who were
sent to collect the church valuables. *Izvestia* declared that, in
preliminary investigations, Tikhon had admitted guilt to
almost all of these charges and that the most famous Soviet
prosecutor Krylenko was assigned to the case, indicating the
great importance the government attached to it.

On April 24, the newspaper printed a special announcement that the trial of Patriarch Tikhon had been postponed to
combine it with that of Bishop Feodosy of Kolomna and that

a special announcement would be made when the trials were to take place. This news was mysterious as many admission tickets to the trial already had been sold.

In May 1923, Tikhon's position became most precarious because of increased hostile attacks by the British press[2] arising from the Curzon ultimatum. Lord Curzon,[3] supported by the Archbishop of Canterbury, had included the patriarch's release from imprisonment in his demands, and this was resented bitterly by the Soviet government. Newspaper editorials promised that Tikhon's own disclosures at the trial would amply justify his imprisonment. The big city papers printed many articles against Tikhon that were purported to be from the lower clergy, Red Army men, peasants, and workers, and then local papers throughout Russia reprinted these articles.

The trial was announced for June 17, but again nothing happened. However, on June 27, the day before the trial was to have taken place, the newspapers published the following statement made by Tikhon to the Supreme Court:

> In making this appeal to the Supreme Court of the RSFSR, I regard it as my duty according to my pastoral conscience to state the following:
>
> Having been raised in a monarchist society and being until my very arrest under the influence of anti-Soviet persons, hostility at times changed from a passive condition to active deeds such as: the proclamation on the subject of the Peace of Brest in 1918, the anathematization of the government in the same year and, finally, the appeal against the removal of church valuables in 1922. All my anti-Soviet acts, except for a few inaccuracies, are set forth in the indictment of the Supreme Court. Recognizing the correctness of the court in bringing me to trial, according to the articles of the Criminal Code indicated in the indictment, I repent of these actions against the state order, and I ask the Supreme Court to change its sentence and to set me free.

At the same time I declare to the Supreme Court
that henceforth I am not an enemy of the Soviet Power. I
am finally and decisively setting myself apart from both
the foreign and the internal monarchist White Guard
counterrevolutionaries.

Signed: Patriarch Tikhon

16 June

(Vasily Bellavin)[4]

Izvestia then announced that, on June 25, the Trial Collegium for Criminal Affairs of the Supreme Court ruled "to
grant the request of Citizen Bellavin to end his retention under
arrest."[5]

About two weeks before the patriarch's confession, he had
been moved from the Donskoy Monastery to one of the Moscow prisons of the GPU called Lubyanka. The patriarch told
a friend, who gave the account to Emhardt, the main reason
for this move.[6] One day around the first of June, during five
o'clock tea the patriarch suddenly began to vomit and then lost
consciousness for a long period of time. His attendants thought
the attack was food poisoning from fish that he had eaten at
his two o'clock dinner, but the patriarch thought it was a slight
attack of apoplexy from irregular digestion and nerves. For
one and one-half hours, he was unconscious and when he came
to his senses, he complained of great weakness and heaviness
in his body on the right side, but this state did not last long.
During the year of imprisonment, the patriarch had aged considerably in appearance and had grown thin.

The Soviets, however, accepted neither the patriarch's nor
his attendants' explanations and, claiming that an attempt at
poisoning might have been made, removed him to the Lubyanka prison. When the announcement of his illness appeared
in *Izvestia*, people began to gather outside the Lubyanka prison
on June 26. Soon the entire square was filled, and then the
people quietly waited. A door opened and there, surrounded

by guards, walked out a disheveled old man with uncombed gray hair and a tangled beard. Only his deep eyes were alive in a face aged and blank with a set expression. He wore an old soldier's coat over his naked body. His feet were bare. When he saw the enormous crowd, tears ran down his face. All knelt before him and so emotional was the atmosphere that even the guards bowed their heads. Repeatedly he blessed the crowds as he made his way back to the Donskoy Monastery. The streets were filled by people who began celebrating as if it were Easter.[7]

A great deal has been written to explain why the Soviets released Tikhon. There was in fact no definite reason, but an accumulation of many reasons. Lenin already had indicated that the Soviets did not wish a martyr to plague them, and certainly Tikhon's death would have had a great psychological power to sway the masses. Although the Curzon ultimatum was resented bitterly, the great stir in the official newspapers indicates how seriously disturbed the government was by British interference and the adverse propaganda being printed in all the British newspapers. As early as May 25, 1922, the Archbishop of Canterbury had raised a question in Parliament concerning the persecution of the Church of Russia, and Metropolitan Evlogy in Paris had written a letter describing the true state of things, which was widely publicized throughout England. The Soviet Ambassador Krasin[8] denied all these accusations categorically and stated that the majority of the clergy were against Tikhon and that only the old sympathizers of the monarchy and capitalism who had lost their position under the new government were faithful to the patriarch. This letter was printed in the *Times* (London) on May 26, 1922. The Archbishop of Canterbury, however, insisted on his accusations and asked to send an unbiased investigating committee to Russia. This Krasin refused. On July 10, 1922, the archbishop gave a public speech in which he again spoke of the trials and killings of the Russian clergy. It was on the basis of this speech that a section of the Curzon ultimatum dealt with the patriarch.

Another aspect of the problem that probably influenced the Soviet government was highlighted by a cartoon that appeared in a Moscow worker's newspaper. The picture showed a hand-to-hand fight between the patriarch and another cleric, presumably a member of the Living Church. At the side was a grinning workman with his hands in his pockets watching the strife. Underneath was printed, "While two are engaged in a struggle, the hands of the third are free."[9] Certainly, the Living Church existed only by the support of the government, for it failed completely to convert the people and only by the aid of the GPU and illegal ousting of the Tikhonite clergy could it, even on paper, show any gains. The Soviet government, however, was against all religion and while giving temporary support to the Living Church to divide and conquer the enemy, it also would permit its unlikely ally to be conquered if it seemed to get too strong.

A final answer to the problem might rest solely in Tikhon's confession. This, if taken seriously, could be offered to the British as justification of the Soviet government's attitude toward the patriarch. It certainly made good propaganda for the government at home and was used as a cloak for all future government arrests of the clergy. It provided a potential threat to all enemies of the state, showing how powerful the new government actually was now that it had vanquished even the last existing monarchist institution.

Certainly, the patriarch's reason for submission is obvious even to his enemies. No one can accuse the patriarch of cowardice for throughout his life he seemed to be fearless as far as personal safety was concerned. On the last day of freedom before his arrest, he came to evening service very late and extremely tired, straight from a long session with the GPU. One of the attendants asked him how "they" were. He answered,

"They were very strict today."

"So what will happen to you"?

"They promised to cut off my little head."

He answered with a smile and proceeded to conduct the rest of the service with no sign of fear. When the priest was about to begin the sermon, the patriarch blessed him and whispered, "Do not provoke them."[10]

The next day the patriarch was arrested.

During Tikhon's imprisonment, he purposely was given to read only the official government papers, which constantly reported in glowing terms the enormous gains made by the Living Church. Gradually, cut off from the outside world, he became convinced that the Church was being ruined, and he realized that the greatest sacrifice must be made; he could not afford to be a martyr, but he must live and save the Church. He once later said to those who questioned: "Let my name perish in history, only that the Church might live."[11]

When the Anglican Bishop Bury questioned the patriarch about his reason for leaving prison, the patriarch reminded him of Paul's words in Philippians 1:23–24: "For I am in a state betwixt two, having a desire to depart, and to be with Christ: which is far better; Nevertheless to abide in the flesh is more needful for you." He said for an old man and a monk to die was too easy. Such heroism would be unheroic in this case. The important thing was the Church. Tikhon later indicated that he regretted leaving prison when he saw how feeble the Living Church really was, but he had no knowledge of this until he was released.

Tikhon always had a feeling of closeness to the people and genuinely loved them. He knew the faithful ones would understand that he did what he had to do to save the Church, and his faith in the people was justified.

Following his release, a representative of the *Guardian* (Manchester) interviewed Tikhon, and even in this official interview, he clearly showed that his confession had not been real. According to the confession, Tikhon said, "I was filled with hostility against the Soviet authorities ... Acknowledging the correctness of the accusation of the Supreme Court ... I repent of all my action against the government ... I am no longer an enemy to the Soviet Government etc." In the interview, however, the patriarch stated the following:

> I have never sought to overthrow the government. In 1918, I stood openly against some of its decrees. I am not a counter-revolutionary, in spite of the fact that some of my appeals had an anti-Soviet character. The power of the Soviet government has greatly increased in Russia; and it has undergone various developments. We, members of the old clergy, are not now struggling against the Soviets, but against the Living Church.
>
> What were the causes of your liberation and the change in the attitude of the Soviet government toward you?
>
> I am persuaded that, having studied my case, the government became convinced that I was no counterrevolutionary. It was suggested that I should make a public declaration of the fact, and I wrote a letter to say so.[12]

Tikhon had signed a pro forma confession and considered it so meaningless that he forgot it and contradicted himself almost at once. Certainly, he could never feel anything but antipathy to a government whose fundamental basis was without God and that did everything it could to persecute the Church and those faithful to her. Yet Tikhon was a man of Christ, and although often urged, he never counseled violent opposition to the government, but only peaceful protection of the Church and what it stood for. Even when the Soviets began to desecrate the relics of St Sergius, he refused to bless a miniature army of 25,000 people who had sworn to protect the relics and instead counseled peace at all costs.

To think of Tikhon as a plotting counterrevolutionary is to misunderstand the man completely. Tikhon was right in attaching no value to the confession, for no one took it seriously.

Another example of this same attitude occurred later when the government forced Tikhon to order prayers to be said in the service for the Soviet government. The order was permitted to remain a dead letter, and the patriarchate churches continued to pray for the "Russian realm" as before.

On July 1,[13] the first Sunday after he was released from prison, Tikhon officiated at the Donskoy Monastery. Great crowds turned up and the patriarch's path was strewn with flowers. So dense was the crowd that the square outside the church was filled, and after the service, the patriarch came out and performed a moleben[14] in the square. For several hours, he remained there, blessing the faithful. During the service, he gave a short talk saying that the Church must keep out of politics, and then he opened his campaign against the Living Church by saying that the Renovationist Council of 1923 could not be recognized, for it was absolutely uncanonical.

On July 15, 1923, from the Donskoy Monastery, the patriarch issued the following message, which was in reality the death knell of the Living Church. It is also interesting as the patriarch's explanation of what had taken place at the fatal meetings more than a year before.

By the grace of God, we, humble Tikhon, patriarch of Moscow and All Russia, to the most reverend bishops, pious priests, and honorable monks and to all faithful children of the Orthodox Church of Russia: God's peace and blessing.

More than a year ago, in consequence of circumstances well known to all, we had been set aside from our pastoral ministry, and have since not been able to stand personally at the helm of the administration to guard the age-hallowed traditions of the Church.

Therefore, as soon as circumstances demanded it, we, strictly conforming to the regulations of the Council which instituted the procedure of patriarchal administration of the Church of Russia, and in compliance with our resolution with the Holy Synod, passed on November 7/20, 1920, we considered it advantageous to transfer the fullness of spiritual authority during the time of our retirement from office, to our Deputy appointed by ourselves, the Metropolitan of Yaroslavl', Agathangel. He was to convoke a second local Council of the Church of Russia for the purpose of organization of the Supreme Ecclesiastical Administration and other needs of the Church. We had been informed that the civil authorities were not opposed to it and Metropolitan Agathangel accepted the task we had charged him with. But for reasons over which he had no control, he was also arrested and could not enter upon the fulfillment of his duties. Ambitious and self-willed individuals made use of it, and "not entering by the door, but climbing up another way" (John 10:1), they usurped the supreme authority over the Orthodox Church of Russia, which did not belong to them.

On May 5/18 of the previous year, during our imprisonment in the Holy Trinity metochion, the priests Vvedensky, Belkov, and Kalinovsky (who but a short time later had renounced the holy orders) visited us, and under the pretext of caring for the welfare of the Church, presented us with a written statement, wherein they complained that in consequence of the existing circumstances, church business remained unattended. They begged us to entrust our chancery to them in order that they may settle the incoming documents in order. Considering this useful, we acceded to their solicitations and inscribed upon their statement the following resolution: "The persons named below (i.e., the priests who signed the letter) are ordered to take over and transmit the synodal business to the Most Reverend Metropolitan Agathangel, upon his arrival in Moscow, with the assistance of Secretary Numerov." According to the meaning of this resolution, they were merely entrusted with taking over the chancery business and to pass them to Metropolitan Agathangel, when he arrived in Moscow. We did not make any arrangements regarding what should they do, if Metropolitan Agathangel will not arrive in Moscow at all, for we could not foresee that possibility at the time. The resolution, however, could not contain the blessing that they themselves should preside over the Ecclesiastical Administration, instead of Metropolitan Agathangel, for the episcopal authority cannot be transferred to presbyters. Nevertheless, this our resolution was declared by them as an act of transferring the authority over the Church to them, and upon the agreement with Bishop Antonin (Granovsky) and Bishop Leonid (Skobeyev), they formed the so-called "Supreme Church Administration." In order to justify their self-willed behaviour, they repeatedly insisted, both in print and at public meetings, that they had entered upon the administration of the Church by an agreement with the patriarch (*Pravda*, May 21, 1922), and that they were members of the Supreme Ecclesiastical Administration "in conformity with the resolution of the Patriarch Tikhon" (Vvedensky, *Revolution and the Church*, 28), and that they "have received from the hands of the patriarch himself the Supreme Ecclesiastical Administration" (*The Living Church*, nos. 4–5, 9). At the meeting held on June 12, 1922, in response to the motion of one of the priests to abstain from any new church reforms without the patriarch's approval, the chairman of the meeting, Bishop Antonin, declared; "As patriarch Tikhon has transmitted his authority to the Supreme Ecclesiastical Administration without reservations, we have no need to run after him to receive from him what he no longer possesses" (*Izvestia*, no. 132, April 16, 1922).

Today we solemnly and within the hearing of all testify from this holy ambo that all these positive statements as to an agreement with us, and as to the transmission of the rights and obligations of the patriarch of the Russian Church to the Supreme Ecclesiastical Administration formed by Bishops Antonin and Leonid, and Priests Vvedensky, Krasnitsky, Kalinovsky, and Belkov, are nothing else but lies and fraud, and that the above-named persons have usurped the ecclesiastical government by seizure and arbitrarily, without any legal authorization established by the rules of our Church. Upon all such persons the Holy Church pronounces a severe judgment. According to canon 16 of the Council of Antioch, a bishop who digresses from the lawful order and arbitrarily invades another bishop's diocese even though requested by all the people to do so, is to be expelled from it and to be degraded from his sacerdotal rank for the sin of infringing the Church laws.

Those persons who have organized the self-styled Supreme Ecclesiastical Administration in Moscow, and are on that account guilty in the eyes of the Church, have further aggravated their position by ordaining bishops to the unlawfully usurped dioceses, and have incurred thereby censure according to the Apostolic canon 31, which threatens to depose from the holy orders those who performed the ordination, as well as him who was himself ordained.

And how have they used the unlawfully usurped ecclesiastical authority? They have used it not for the building up of the Church, but in sowing seeds of a destructive schism: in depriving Orthodox bishops of their sees for having remained faithful to their duty and for refusing to submit to them; in persecuting the reverend priests, who in accordance with the canons of the Church have not submitted themselves to them, they have founded everywhere the so-called "Living Church," which despises the authority of the Universal Church and strives to impair the necessary Church discipline, in order to secure victory to its own party and to carry out by force its objectives without heeding the catholic voice of all the believers.

By all these actions, they have separated themselves from the body of the Universal Church and deprived themselves of God's grace which subsists only in the Church of Christ. Consequently, all arrangements made during our absence by those ruling the Church, since they had neither legal nor canonical authority, are null and void, and all actions and sacraments performed by bishops and clergymen who have forsaken the Church, are devoid of the grace of God, while the faithful taking part in such prayers and sacraments shall receive no sanctification thereby, and are subject to condemnation for participation in their sin.

Our heart has suffered acutely when the sad news about the Church disorders which have arisen after our retirement has reached us, as we have heard of the violence exercised by the unauthorized, self-imposed "Living Church" government; of the rise of party strife; of the spirit of animosity and division reigning where the spirit of love and brotherly unity should have ruled.

But as long as we had not regained our liberty, we could do nothing to assist in pacifying the Church and allaying the ruinous strife, save to pray in the secrecy of our cell. Now since we have been released from prison and have become fully acquainted with the state of Church affairs, we again assume the primatial authority which we had temporarily transferred to our Deputy, Metropolitan Agathangel, who however, for reasons over which he had no control, had not been able to exercise it. Resuming the exercise of our pastoral duties, we fervently pray to the Master of the Church, our Lord Jesus Christ, to grant us strength and wisdom to govern His Church and to instill into it the spirit of peace, love, and concord. At the same time we call upon all bishops, priests, and faithful sons of the Church, who remained true to their duty, and have bravely defended the divinely established order of the life of the Church, begging them to help us in the task of pacifying the Church by their advice, their labours, and especially their prayers to God the Creator and Sustainer of all. We beseech those that consciously or unconsciously, knowingly or ignorantly, have been seduced by the wiles of the present age and, having acknowledged the unlawful authority, have fallen away from the unity of the Church and the grace of God, to confess their sin, to cleanse themselves by repentance, and to return to the saving bosom of the one Universal Church.

May the blessing of God be with all of you, through the prayers of the Theotokos and the Ever-Virgin Mary, and of our holy fathers, Peter, Alexis, Jonah, Philip, Hermogen, the hierarchs of Moscow and miracle-workers, and all the saints of the Russian land who for ages have been pleasing to God, Amen.

Humble Tikhon
Patriarch of Moscow and All Russia
July 15, 1923[15]

During the patriarch's imprisonment, workers' families had been moved into his apartment at the Donskoy Monastery, but when the Soviets released him, an order was given to clear out his old quarters. He returned to the monastery and moved into three small, simple rooms, one of which was his official reception room. Only the simplest and most necessary furnishings were there. That these three rooms were uncomfortable and badly heated was one of the main reasons Tikhon was forced to go to Dr Bakunin's hospital, not only for treatment, but also to rest in a comfortable, warm place. Whenever he left to serve in an outside church, he was driven in a small cab with one attendant. As before, he was accessible to all, and pilgrims crowded the monastery from across Russia for just a glimpse of his aged, yet peaceful, face. Although people knew the patriarch was weak, they would not leave him alone, and he refused no one.

Daily from nine to twelve o'clock, he received callers at the Donskoy Monastery, and he officiated at services in various Moscow churches every afternoon as well as all day on Saturday and Sunday.

The tradesmen of Moscow kept him supplied with food and drink and refused to accept payment. The women parishioners cleaned and washed his clothing. One of the Living Churchmen suggested that similar free services should be granted to their leaders, but the tradesmen refused to "even sell food to those bastards."[16]

As soon as the patriarch left prison, he at once gathered the reigns of power into his hands. Just before his release, the Tikhonites had been able to hold only five of the Moscow churches, but with his release, the churches, one after another, begged to be restored to the old jurisdiction.[17] Tikhon insisted that all of the renegade churches must be reblessed, and those clergymen who through choice or fear had gone over to the Living Church must repent publicly.[18] Each day, Tikhon presided at the services in the various churches, and at these churches priests and bishops publicly recanted[19] to the patriarch and prayed for the forgiveness of the people. They were then blessed and taken back into the fold.

By the beginning of 1925, the formerly triumphant Living Church, which had in May 1922 been about to sweep away the patriarch and all his followers, was a lingering defensive movement. In vain, through reorganization, hints of reunion, change of name, and shelving of its radical program of married bishops, it tried with the aid of the Soviets to keep control of the religious institutions of Russia, but each year it grew less and less important.

Although the Living Church danger receded from the immediate horizon, the hostility of the government continued both openly and in a veiled fashion. Agents of the GPU constantly were visiting the patriarch and having long private conversations. On numerous occasions, concessions were promised if the patriarch would reciprocate. This constant pressure, added to the threat of the Living Church, occasionally made Tikhon waver. It seemed important to the government to have the Church go on the new calendar, and Tikhon was asked repeatedly to order this change. On July 30, 1923, the patriarch issued a decree changing the Church calendar.[20] As soon as this was issued, a GPU agent provocateur began to visit the various bishops in Moscow asking why the patriarch had changed the calendar and hinting that through senility he was putting the Church into the hands of the government.[21] Reaction to this decree was so strong at the parish level, where people believed that the Living Church had taken over, that Tikhon soon annulled the decree. Many of the patriarch's closest assistants were arrested on the usual counterrevolutionary charges, and through pressure, Tikhon was forced to put an agent of the secret police on the council. This situation became so unpleasant that Tikhon eventually disbanded the entire council to ensure that no organization near him was infiltrated with Bolshevik agents.

Time and time again an agent appeared with a paper for the patriarch to sign, which was to be sent to the Archbishop of Canterbury, denying all Church persecution in Russia. Each time, the patriarch delayed and then a new form of obstruction began. Whenever Tikhon would appoint a bishop to any place in Russia, by accident, he would be sent to the wrong diocese. This happened so often that Tikhon began to joke about it claiming that every time he sent a bishop north, he went south, and when he assigned a bishop to a diocese in the west, he inevitably arrived in the east. But still he did not sign the paper.[22]

The Bolsheviks tried yet another scheme: a paper was drawn up to be signed by Tikhon, which declared that the Orthodox Church was converted legally into the Bolshevik state church. The whole document based on the church canons would have placed the Orthodox Church completely under the state power. The paper was again and again brought forth, particularly as the physical condition of the patriarch grew weaker.[23] The patriarch became increasingly subject to fainting spells preceded and followed by intense trembling. Soon the very announcement of the agent's name, Tuchkov, made the patriarch begin to tremble, but he never refused to see him and always saw him alone, bearing the whole ordeal on his own shoulders.

Priests and bishops throughout Russia continued to be arrested and sentenced to prison or exiled, either on moral or political charges as well as on charges of hiding church valuables. In January 1924, fifteen churchmen of the Lavra of the Caves, one of the most famous old monasteries in Kiev, were arrested. The police claimed that, hidden in the cellars, they had found precious stones, gold, and silver, along with counterrevolutionary correspondence with Patriarch Tikhon, Metropolitan Antony, and other known anti-Soviet churchmen. Again the newspapers began the hue and cry about the "former patriarch Tikhon,"[24] who was supposed to have authority over the Lavra. Tikhon was forced to deny publicly any knowledge or complicity in the concealment of the valuables in a letter to *Izvestia*, adding the following:

> We have not been and are not in communication with foreign counterrevolutionaries, nor with counterrevolutionary groups within the USSR, and we do not know anything about the counterrevolutionary political work' of the monks of the Lavra.[25]

Possibly as a result of this, in March 1924, the government dropped the pending case against the patriarch, an action that neither cleared nor convicted him. The government explanation said that his public repentance and the widespread mass movement away from religion to science by the workers and peasants showed[26] that the patriarch and his cohorts were no longer "socially dangerous."[27] The expression "socially dangerous" demonstrates the government's real charge against the patriarch when it was stripped of all the trimmings of counterrevolutionary, anti-Soviet words.

On August 26(o.s.), 1924, the patriarch celebrated his last namesday.[28] All day, delegations visited him with gifts, including manufacturers, growers, gardeners, and market committees, and all had personal interviews. From America,[29] a Russian–American delegation came and spoke of the great love of the Orthodox Americans for him and their happy memories of his years there. Kneeling, the delegation presented him with a golden miter studded with diamonds and robes of dark green velvet with a satin and gold thread border.

On December 22, 1924, a second attempt on the life of the patriarch was made. For many years, the patriarch had been served by a man called Yakov Anisimovich Polozov. Yakov had been with him during his years in America, and then on returning to Russia had married Princess Drutskaya-Sokolinskaya. When Tikhon became patriarch, Yakov was again with him, probably the closest person to him throughout those harrowing years. On the evening of December 22, the patriarch was standing before the icons in his bedroom praying. Hearing a shot, he crossed himself in the direction of the shot and then opened the door. For a moment, the door could not be opened for something was obstructing it. It suddenly gave way, and there Yakov lay covered with blood, half on the floor and half against the door. Two men stood before the patriarch. On seeing him, one of them grabbed a fur coat from the hanger and, turning, ran out. The other followed, also running. Tikhon shouted, "Stop, what have you done? You have killed a man!" Yakov opened his eyes, looked at the patriarch, and then died. The police were called at once, and the next day a notice was printed in *Izvestia* that two thieves had entered the apartment of citizen Bellavin and stolen a fur coat. No mention was made of the murder and no investigation ever was made.[30] Curiously enough, the Bolsheviks made an issue over

Yakov's burial. The patriarch wished to have him buried at the monastery, and for a while, the Bolsheviks refused. Finally it was allowed, but almost as soon as the grave was made, the government announced that they were building a crematorium on that spot. Tikhon had the grave removed next to the walls of the church, and his own body was to be placed in the grave next to Yakov's. This incident shattered the patriarch's little remaining health, and his angina attacks increased.

On January 12, 1925, the patriarch's doctor told him that he must be hospitalized for complete rest and quiet. The patriarch at last consented, but the first hospital refused to take him as a patient fearing the responsibility of such a controversial key figure. A small private hospital run by Drs Bakunins, a married couple, offered to take Tikhon. On January 13, an attendant drove Tikhon and he was accompanied only by the son of a close friend. Dr Bakunina admitted him and described him as an old, gray, skinny man, who was highly nervous but never complained. He was suffering from a severe attack of sclerosis, chronic inflammation of the kidneys, and increasingly severe angina attacks. On February 23, 1924, he had another severe attack of sclerosis, and although the doctors tried to hospitalize him, the patriarch, through sheer will power, had recovered and continued his struggle with the Living Church, which at that time had reached a crucial point.[31] By the following year, however, the strain of his responsibility and increasing illness and the shock of Yakov's murder forced the patriarch to enter the Bakunin Hospital, where he remained for almost three months.

For the first two weeks of his hospital stay, the patriarch was treated with enforced quiet, warm baths, and internal medicine, and from this regime he showed a marked improvement. He lived in a small bright room that had one window overlooking the garden of the Convent of the Conception of the Theotokos. As the spring came on, he took much pleasure in watching the rebirth of the green foliage in nature and the return of the birds. He had brought his own icons, which were hung on the walls, and a lampada[32] constantly was lit. The room contained a leather armchair, a desk, bed, and curtains on the window, and a picture of two little boys standing on a bridge hung on the wall. During the day, Tikhon began to read Turgenev, Goncharov, and the letters of Pobedonostsev. When dressed in his patriarchal garments, the patriarch made an imposing picture, but in bed with only the hospital nightclothes, he became a small shrunken old man. Most of the time, a monk stayed with him, and for the first fortnight all visitors were kept out. Soon the patriarch was exchanging jokes with the doctors, and news of his improvement traveled outside the hospital. At once Tuchkov, Tikhon's particular GPU torturer, appeared. At first Dr Bakunina was able to stave him off, but by the third week, the agent began making long calls on the patriarch, always being closeted with him alone. Tuchkov, as a person, was a rough, half-intelligent peasant. He was extremely talkative and overbearing in his manner.

Those who loved him soon began visiting, but they selfishly demanded too much of his time and greatly fatigued him. Metropolitan Peter often came for long visits; workers' deputations, Yakov Polozov's widow, and even patients at the hospital, for little or no reason, all wanted to see the patriarch, mostly just to be reassured that he was still living. Gifts began pouring in, and a shoemakers' deputation gave him special leather boots interlined with rabbit fur, which gave him the greatest pleasure. He tried them on and off and then began to wear them constantly. The doctors at the hospital constantly counseled rest. In answering this, Tikhon remarked that after his death he would have plenty of time to lie down, but until then, there was work to be done. Again, he began to serve in churches, and when Dr Bakunina remonstrated with him over the coldness of the weather, the patriarch would point to his warm boots and the new warm vestments that had been presented to him during his illness. Soon Tuchkov's visits were supplemented by visits of another GPU agent. It was Tuch-kov's mission to make the patriarch retire, and he kept trying to persuade him to sign the document turning the church into a state church, to retire, and to live in the south of Russia for his health. The second agent would attempt to bribe the patriarch with promises of increased privileges for the church, cancella-tion of prison sentences for churchmen, and so on, and when that failed, the agent would make open threats. The agents always conducted their interviews with Tikhon privately and for many hours at a time. After each interview, Tikhon would be completely exhausted and show signs of nervousness and trembling. After one of these ordeals, Tikhon had gone to bed, but on hearing about a woman patient in the same hos-pital who had become hysterical before an operation, insisted on rising and going to her with prayers and words of comfort.

During Tikhon's stay at the Lubyanka prison, he had come in contact with Dr M. R. Zhizhilenko. After his release, the friendship between the two men continued, and Zhizhilenko came to see him at the hospital. During the last three months, Tikhon became more and more concerned over the position of the church after his death. The constant pressure of Tuchkov and his assistant made him realize how determined the Bolshe-viks were to gain control of the Church. Seeing that the attacks of the Living Church seemed only to strengthen the Tik-honites, Tikhon saw that they were trying to worm their way into and conquer the Orthodox organization. They already had succeeded in placing an agent on the highest Church coun-cil who had disorganized the council's work to such a degree that Tikhon was obliged to disband the entire council. Tikhon knew he had the strength not to sign over the Church to the Bolsheviks,[33] but would others, after him, be able to see the clear path, or might they waver, as he himself had occasion-ally wavered? During his conversation with Zhizhilenko, he voiced these fears, and shortly before his death, he said that the only way for the Church to remain loyal to Christ probably was to go into the catacombs. At one of these meetings, Tikhon secretly blessed Zhizhilenko to enter monasticism with the command that should the higher clergy later betray Christ and give up the Church's spiritual freedom,[34] Zhizhilenko was to lead the Church into the catacombs. This foresight of Tikhon's proved correct, and before the 1920s were over, Zhizhilenko became the first secret catacomb bishop of Serpukhov, Maxim.

An encouraging sign of increasing good health for the patriarch was the complete absence of angina attacks during his three months' stay at the hospital. At the beginning of Lent, Tikhon served for five days at the Donskoy Monastery, but he returned to the hospital in a state of exhaustion. He complained of a toothache and a dentist was called in. Examination revealed two bad teeth that the dentist then pulled. His gums immediately swelled and the swelling would not abate. The swelling traveled to his throat, and he had great difficulty swallowing and eating. He insisted on serving at a church, but he was so ill he could barely make the responses. A specialist on throat diseases was called in but found nothing wrong.

On March 25 (o.s.), the hospital consulted throat specialists a second time, but again they found nothing serious. That morning in spite of the pain and discomfort, Tikhon passed his time writing business letters. In the evening, Metropolitan Peter came and spent more than two hours with the patriarch. He left the patriarch in an excited way and carried a paper in his hands. The patriarch then left his bedroom and asked for morphine to deaden the pain. An attendant seeing him move his hands strangely, as he had formerly done before the nervous fits that preceded angina attacks, asked him to lie down. The patriarch said he would lie down later, took the morphine, and seemed to grow quieter. About ten o'clock in the evening, the patriarch asked for his washstand and then in a severe voice said, "Now I will fall fast asleep and for long—the night will be long, long, dark, dark." He went to bed and after a while asked his attendant to tie up his jaw, for it bothered him, but the nurse explained that he would be unable to breath, so Tikhon acquiesced and said no more. For a short time, he seemed to sleep. Then he asked for Dr Shchelkan. At this request, both Drs Bakunina and Shchelkan came. Dr Shchelkan felt the slowness of the patriarch's pulse and signaled to the nurse that he was dying. The patriarch looked up and asked, "What time is it?"

"Eleven forty-five," answered the doctor.

"Thank God," the patriarch answered and began to cross himself the traditional three times saying "Glory be to God. Glory be to God, Glory ...," and he died.[35] The patriarch, in fact, was set to be released from the hospital the very next day.

As soon as the patriarch died, Dr Bakunina telephoned Metropolitan Peter to come to the hospital, but before Peter could arrive, the GPU agent Tuchkov arrived. Ever since the patriarch had entered the hospital, all telephone lines to the hospital had been tapped by the GPU for any news of him. Tuchkov arrived in a jubilant mood, and seeing the patriarch's body remarked, "That was a good old man, we must bury him rather solemnly."[36] He then proceeded to make a thorough examination of the patriarch's body paying particular attention to his throat and looking for marks of strangulation. He proceeded to question the doctors and attendants minutely, asking what medicine had been administered, what last-minute aid had been given, and so on. By Tikhon's bedside was a small basket containing four thousand rubles, which had ben collected by various parishes to build a special, well-constructed, comfortable house for him at the Donskoy Monastery. This was pocketed by Tuchkov with the remark, "This might be useful for us," and was never after accounted for. When it was suggested that Tikhon's body should be removed to a nearby church until the morning and then taken to the Donskoy Monastery, Tuchkov refused and immediately ordered an ambulance, saying that a hearse should not be used for fear of creating incidents. The body was thus placed in a truck and, attended by Metropolitan

Peter, removed to Tikhon's own cell in the monastery on the outskirts of Moscow. Tuchkov, meanwhile, sealed the room at the hospital and several days later returned and listed everything that had been left in the patriarch's last abode.

On Wednesday morning at five o'clock, the body of the patriarch, dressed in velvet episcopal vestments, arrived at the Donskoy Monastery accompanied by Metropolitan Peter (Poliansky) of Krutitsy and Bishop Boris (Rukin) of Mozhaisk. Slowly and majestically, the great bell of the monastery tolled forty times, announcing the passing of the head of the All-Russian Orthodox Church. Services began in all the churches, and the flag of the foreign embassies flew at half-mast.[37]

On March 27, o. s., the liturgy of St John Chrysostom was celebrated, and the body of the patriarch was carried from its cell into the church and then carried around three times. At this minute, a ray of sunlight caught the body clothed in a gold robe with a dark green velvet border embroidered with icons and gold thread. On his head was the episcopal miter, in his hands were the cross and the Gospel, and by his sides, the subdeacons were holding two and three stick candelabra,[38] as if the Patriarch was blessing the people. Then, as he was lowered into an oak coffin, the deacon intoned, "Thus shone thy light before men and all saw thy good deeds and glorified our Father who is in Heaven." At precisely this moment, the sun disappeared and the impression made on the people was most profound.

The oak coffin was placed on a platform in the middle of the church and was covered with the blue velvet mantle of Patriarch Nikon. Tropical plants were arranged around the coffin, and either side of the dais had enough room for two people to pass through both aisles. Two deacons stood at the head of the coffin next to several large wreaths, one of which was from the Archbishop of Canterbury. When the time for the sermon came, a bishop entered the church and, in official language, announced the death of the eleventh patriarch of Russia and asked for the mourning crowd to refrain from incidents.

He said that all would be able to have a farewell view of the patriarch, but he was responsible for their good behavior. He begged the people to make no demonstration of feeling, or all would be in trouble. Then he went out onto the porch of the church and made the same announcement to the tightly packed crowd. The entire yard was filled with an estimated 150,000 people, and when the line was formed of four people at a time, it stretched back for more than a mile. The clergy first passed by the bier, four abreast, until they reached the coffin, and then split into two lines on either side of the dais. Each one knelt, kissing the cross, gospel, and vestments of the patriarch, and then quietly went into the yard on the north side of the church. The people followed slowly. Attendants appeared, wearing black armbands with white crosses, but during the entire day, no incident of any kind occurred. One woman fainted and was at once borne out by a waiting nurse. Approximately 100 to 120 people passed by every minute, and the procession continued until the last person passed the coffin.

The burial service took place on March 30 (o.s.), 1925. The enormous crowd in the yard, the streets, in the monastery, on trees, on the turrets of the churches, and everywhere else that people could stand or perch, all joined in singing "Hosanna"[39] and "Eternal Memory." Bells rang across Moscow, and every church conducted individual services. When the coffin was carried from its resting place, the people rushed to kiss the spot where it had lain. Slowly the coffin was carried through the monastery buildings to the so-called warm church where it was buried in the ground. An oak cross was raised above the grave, which read:

Tikhon, Most Holy Patriarch of Moscow and All Russia.
25 March, 1925, o.s.

During his tenure in North America, Bishop Tikhon (Bellavin) signed this photograph for Theodore Nemirsky. Inscription: "Bishop Tikhon, Wostok, Canada, 1901, Aug. 21. To Theodore Nemirsky." (Source: Holy Trinity Seminary Archives, Foundation of Russian History)

An oil-painting of the Most Holy Patriarch Tikhon of Moscow and All Russia by Archimandrite Cyprian (Pyzhov) (Source: Holy Trinity Monastery, Jordanville, New York)

The burial service of His Holiness Patriarch Tikhon took place on March 30 (o.s.), 1925. Enormous crowds processed past the funeral bier for their farewell view. (Source: Holy Trinity Monastery, Jordanville, New York)

In February 1992 the relics of St Tikhon were discovered concealed under the floor of the lesser cathedral in the Donskoy Monastery. His body was almost entirely incorrupt. (Source: Православная беседа, issue 2-3, 1992, www.p-beseda.ru. Scan from Trinity Seminary Archives, Foundation of Russian History)

СТЫЙ ТѴХѠНЪ   ПАТРІАРХЪ

Icon of Saint Tikhon, Patriarch of Moscow (Source: Holy Trinity Monastery, Jordanville, New York)

CHAPTER 6

The Will

Several days after the burial of the patriarch, *Izvestia* announced that it had received the following letter along with the will of Patriarch Tikhon:

> The Editorial Office of *Izvestia*.
>
> Citizen Editor:
>
> We beg that you do not refuse space in your paper *Izvestia* to the enclosed proclamation of Patriarch Tikhon, signed by him on April 7, 1925.
>
> Peter (Poliansky), Metropolitan of Krutitsy
>
> Tikhon (Obolensky), Metropolitan of the Urals
>
> April 14, 1925[1]

Izvestia of course, was delighted to publish the following will supposedly written by the patriarch and given to Metropolitan Peter the night that he died:

> By the grace of God, humble Tikhon, the patriarch of Moscow and all the Russian Church.
>
> Grace and peace from our Lord and Saviour, Jesus Christ.
>
> During the years of the great upheaval, in accordance with the will of God without which nothing happens in this world, the Soviet government became the head of the Russian state and took upon itself a heavy responsibility— the removal of burdensome consequences of the bloody war and of the terrible famine.

Entering upon the administration of the Russian state, the representatives of the Soviet power issued, in January, 1918, a decree concerning the full liberty of the citizens to believe as they please and to live in accordance with that faith. In such manner, the principle of liberty of conscience, affirmed by the Constitution of the USSR, guaranteed to every religious society, including also our Orthodox Church, the right as well as the possibility to live and to conduct its religious affairs in conformity with the demands of its faith, so long as this does not infringe upon public order and the rights of other citizens. Therefore, we have acknowledged to the whole nation, in its time, in our messages to the hierarchs, priests, and their flocks, the new order of affairs as well as the people's government of workers and peasants, whose authority we sincerely welcomed.

It is time that the believers understand the Christian point of view that "the destiny of nations is directed by the Lord," and to accept all that has come to pass as the expression of the will of God. Without sinning against our faith or Church, without surrendering anything of them—in a word, without permitting any compromises or concessions in the realm of belief, as citizens, we must be sincere in our attitude toward the Soviet government and the labors of the USSR for general welfare, condemning all association with the enemies of the Soviet government and all open or secret agitation against it.

Offering our prayers for the outpouring of God's blessings on the labors of the nations which have united their forces in the name of common good, we call upon all beloved members of the God-protected Church of Russia in these responsible times of upbuilding of the common welfare of the nation, to unite with us in a fervent prayer to the Most High God for granting aid to the government of workers and peasants in its labors for the good of all the people. We call upon the parish communities, and especially upon their executive bodies, not to admit any machinations of ill-meaning persons against the government, not to nurture hopes for the restoration of the monarchical system, but to become convinced that the Soviet government is actually the people's government of workers and peasants, and hence durable and stable. We make an appeal that worthy people, honorable and devoted to the Orthodox Church, not meddling in politics and sincerely loyal to the Soviet government, be chosen for parochial councils. The activity of the Orthodox communities must not be directed to the political game, which is utterly foreign to the Church of God, but to the strengthening of the Orthodox faith, for the enemies of the holy Orthodoxy—i.e., sectarians, Catholics, Protestants, renovationists, atheists and the like—endeavour to use every opportunity which offers itself in the life of the Orthodox Church for injuring her. The enemies of the Church adopt all kinds of deceit, compulsion, as well as bribery, in their efforts to reach their goal. It suffices to look upon the events in Poland, where out of the three hundred and fifty churches and monasteries existing there, only fifty are left. The rest were either closed or turned into Catholic churches, not to mention those persecutions to which our Orthodox clergy was subjected.

Now by the grace of God, having regained health, again entering upon the service of the Church of God, we call upon you, beloved brethren-hierarchs and priests, once more condemning all opposition to the government, as well as all evil-intentioned project, sedition, and all hatred of the government, to share with us in our work for pacification of our flock and for edification of the Church of God.

In deference to the duty incumbent upon us to guard the purity of church life, seeking first of all the salvation of men and the realization in life of the eternal divine principles, we cannot but condemn those who, in forgetfulness of the divine ends, misuse their ecclesiastical position by giving themselves beyond measure to the human—and often degrading—political game, sometimes even of a criminal character. Therefore, in accordance with the duty of our office as primate, we approve of appointing a special commission to be charged with the investigation, and if deemed proper, even removal from office, in accordance with the canonical order, of those hierarchs and priests who persist in their delusions and refuse to manifest a repentance of them before the Soviet government, and to bring such before the judgment of the Orthodox Council.

At the same time, we must mention with a deep sorrow that certain sons of Russia, and even hierarchs and priests, have left the motherland for various reasons, and already have busied themselves in activities to which they have not been called and which in any case are injurious to our Church. Making use of our name and our ecclesiastical authority, they have carried on harmful and counterrevolutionary activity. We positively declare that we have no connection with them, as our enemies affirm: they are strangers to us, and we condemn their harmful activity. They have freedom of conviction, but they use our name and the name of the holy Church in an unauthorized fashion and against the canons of our Church, feigning to be solicitous about its good. The so-called Council of Karlovtsy brougth no blessing to the Church or the people, and we again confirm its condemnation, and hold it necessary to proclaim firmly and positively that any such further attempt will call forth on our part extreme measures, even to the suspension in sacred duties and judgment by the Council. In order to avoid such severe penalties, we call upon all hierarchs and priests abroad to cease their political activity in connection with the enemies of our nation, and to have the courage to return to the motherland and to speak the truth about themselves and the Church of God.

Their activity should be investigated. They should give an account of themselves to the Orthodox ecclesiastical conscience. We order that a special commission should investigate the activity of the hierarchs and priests who have fled abroad, and especially of Metropolitan Anthony (Khrapovitzky), formerly of Kiev, Metropolitan Platon (Rozhdestvensky), formerly of Odessa, as well as others, and immediately to prepare a statement concerning their activity. Their refusal to submit to our demand will oblige us to judge them in their absence.

Our enemies, endeavoring to separate us from our beloved children, the priests entrusted us by God, are spreading lying rumors that we are not at liberty in our patriarchal office to speak freely, and even are not free in conscience; that we are controlled by the presumptive enemies of the people and deprived of the possibility of having communication with the flock we lead. We declare all such inventions regarding our lack of freedom to be lies and seduction, for there is no government upon the earth which could bind our hierarchal conscience or our patriarchal word. Fearlessly and trustfully looking toward the future course of the holy Orthodoxy, we humbly beseech you, our beloved children, to guard the work of God, and the powers of lawlessness will have no success.

Calling God's blessing upon the hierarchs, priests, and children who are faithful to us, we beseech you with a peaceful conscience, without fear of sinning against the holy faith, submit yourselves to the Soviet government not out of fear, but because of conscience, remembering the words of the Apostle: "Let every soul be obedient to those who rule over them; for there is no government, but is ordained of God ... and the governments that be, are of God" (Rom 13:1).

At the same time we express a firm belief that the establishment of pure and sincere relations will prompt our government to deal with us with full confidence, and will give us the possibility to teach our children the law of God, to open theological schools for the training of priesthood, and to publish books and journals in defense of the Orthodox faith.

May the Lord strengthen you all in devotion to the Orthodox faith, Church, and its hierarchy.

Patriarch Tikhon
Donskoy Monastery
April 7, 1925[2]

This sensational will has become one of the most controversial documents. Historians are completely divided in their views. Some believe it to be bona fide, some believe it be a forgery on the part of the Soviets, and others think it to be a forgery on the part of Peter of Krutitsy to strengthen his shaky position. J. S. Curtiss has taken the attitude that Tikhon completely reversed his anti-Soviet attitude and became a firm supporter of the godless government. He quotes as proof the evaluation of Petr Smidovich, one of the darkest figures among the Soviets, and therefore accepts the will as a genuine expression of Tikhon's reversed position.[3] He seems to have overlooked certain important facts, however.

Early apologists for Tikhon attempted to challenge the will because of its dating. The will was dated according to the new style. Certainly, the Patriarch had gone through much trouble over this and had come to realize how firmly the Russian people associated the new style with the Living Church movement. It is difficult to imagine that he would date a document that he wished to reach and influence all the Orthodox in a way that immediately would antagonize them. He would have been the first to realize that anything so dated would immediately arouse suspicion in everyone's mind as to its authenticity. Also, the will had given the Donskoy Monastery as the place where it was written, and yet Tikhon had been at the Bakunin Hospital. This could be explained easily, however, by the fact that all arrangements had been made for Tikhon to leave the

hospital on the following day and to return to the monastery where the document, if real, would have been issued as
a proclamation. It was called a will only because the patriarch
had died.

The very contents of the document leave one filled with
doubt. Why should Tikhon write such a document? There
was really no reason. He said nothing new, and he provided
no real instructions to the people. He already had said several
times that the clergy should stay out of politics and that since
nothing happened without the will of God, the Soviet government must be accepted. The attacks against the Protestants,
Catholics, Poles, and sectarians were not real and could not
fool the believing Orthodox who were quite aware who the
true enemy of the church was.

The whole document seems pointless and unnecessary. It is
only when one places one's frame of reference into the Bolshevik psychology that one can understand the will. The Soviet
government could benefit from it, for by the contents of the
document, Tikhon seemed to bless the government, condemn
all its enemies (from the Karlovtsy Synod to the Polish nation-
alists), and surrender the whole policy of Church relations with
the government into Bolshevik hands. The whole document is
cleverly worded from this viewpoint, for by listing a few of the
Church grievances at the end, it gives the implication of a hidden bribe to the people, if the will is preserved.

The final and masterful stroke was to print that the document had been sent by Peter of Krutitsy and Tikhon of the
Urals, but this was the biggest slip of all. First, neither of
the two churchmen ever confirmed the claim of *Izvestia* that
they had sent the document. The letter printed from the two
churchmen says, "the enclosed proclamation of Patriarch Tikhon, signed by him on April 7, 1925." Halfway through the
document, we find these words, "Now we by grace of God,
having regained health, again entering upon the services of the
Church of God." This statement is in complete contradiction

of affairs as they stood on April 7, and yet this is when, according to *Izvestia*'s note from Peter and Tikhon, the patriarch signed the document. On April 7, Tikhon was but a few hours from death and was almost completely incapacitated by a swollen throat and gums and by the beginning symptoms of an approaching heart attack. To write or sign a document speaking of his returned health was ridiculous. Also, during his illness, the patriarch had relinquished his "services of the Church of God," and so to speak of again entering upon them was to distort the real state of affairs, and Tikhon could have had no purpose for doing this.

Professor Ivan Andreyev,[4] a preeminent historian of the Russian Church, after a careful examination of all documents known to have been written by the patriarch, has pointed out two other glaring errors that appear to provide conclusive evidence that the document was forged. They are precisely the type of errors that a forger would make.

The beginning of the decree is, "By the grace of God, humble Tikhon, the patriarch of Moscow and all the Russian Church." This is apparently a completely distorted beginning of the original, "By the grace of God, humble Tikhon, the patriarch of Moscow and all Russia," and one that would never be and never was used by the patriarch on Church decrees. Tikhon, as all patriarchs, always was styled "all Russia," assuming that all Russia was Orthodox and not just the Church. This assumption would be precisely the sort of thing known to all churchmen but forgotten or overlooked by a Bolshevik. The second error came in the signature. Throughout the seven years of his patriarchal office, Tikhon never referred to himself or signed his name in any other way than, "the humble Tikhon." His way of living, his lack of self-feeling, his absorbed devotion to the Virgin, and his feeling that he was only a simple vessel to be used at his Lord's commandment would have made it impossible for him to sign himself "Patriarch Tikhon" and assume the pomp and authority of such a signature.

On December 25 (o.s.), 1924, Tikhon, realizing that his end was approaching, in a short simple document had turned over his authority to Metropolitan Kirill, Metropolitan Agathangel, and Metropolitan Peter as his choice for the post of *locum tenens*. The understanding was that a new council was to be held within forty days of the patriarch's death. Such an act showed clearly that Tikhon was preparing for death and attempting to leave his church in as good order as it could be in the existing circumstances. The so-called will with its new style dating, Bolshevik-flavored advice, and peculiar signature could not be the act of a dying man attempting to strengthen and unify his people and guide them in their relations with the two warring worlds of the present materialism and future spirituality.

* * *

It is difficult to assess the greatness of Tikhon. Certainly, his spiritual growth was far beyond that of the ordinary mortal. One of the most striking peculiarities of his character was an absolute necessity for the patriarch constantly to be conducting liturgies, a duty for which so many bishops had little time. Throughout his life from the time he became a monk, Tikhon went out of his way to take part in services either in his own church or as a visiting priest to another church. When he became metropolitan of Moscow, people were at first confused by the appearance of such a high dignitary constantly officiating in one church or another, seldom missing a day. He would not recognize bodily discomfort as an impediment to his priestly serving, and his intense spiritual development was felt easily by the people, all the more since he dispensed with the usual formal manner and ceremony normally associated with high church dignitaries. His habit of traveling almost unattended, quietly bowing and blessing all who approached, was not only unique, but, in the revolutionary times, precisely what was needed to disprove the Bolshevik picture of the fat selfish monk concerned only with his own importance and the church possessions for his use. It was precisely the "humble Tikhon," as he signed himself, who was the right man for that critical hour.

It was probably not, however, Tikhon's great spiritual power that made him so beloved, but rather the tremendous warmth and humaneness of his personality. No one was afraid to approach him, and the humblest Siberian pilgrim had the same access to him, the same personal interview, as a visiting archbishop from America. He truly possessed an unblemished character, and yet this is often the thing that would make for hate rather than love, for jealousy and sarcasm rather than affection. Purity of character usually is appreciated only after death. Along with this high-minded nature, however, Tikhon possessed a great and never failing sense of humor and a warmth of manner that was immediately felt not only by his intimates but by the crowd at large. He loved people, loved to talk with them, and loved to entertain them, and like all Russians, he loved to drink tea and visit late into the night. He could not be provoked into losing his temper even when baited, for example, by the prosecutor at the Moscow Trial of the Fifty-Four. His constant theme was that all the Russian people had sinned and forgotten their Lord—not just one group, not just one philosophy was responsible; Russia as a whole was being punished for her own transgressions and must suffer the punishment to be purified. He clearly felt that God's wrath had been provoked, and therefore Tikhon could blame no one person or group but constantly exhorted all to stop their sinning and return to God. His exhortations were not based on anger but rather on love, and this was so clearly shown by the way he welcomed back with kisses those repenters who had done both him and the Church the worst harm during the critical year from 1922 to 1923.

Thus, Patriarch Tikhon, born Vasily Ivanovich Bellavin, lived and died. Since his death, the Church has suffered much, and yet it continues. Many of the clergy went underground, and during the retreat of the Germans in 1942, thousands of Russians came out bearing tales of wandering priests, secret councils of bishops, and a burning faith that no GPU, no new materialism, and no scientific "truth" had been able to kill. So strong was this faith that an official church was erected during World War II to administer to the permitted spiritual demands of the people, but the Tikhonite underground movement continued as an outlawed but flourishing institution. To the present day, the Tikhon's grave still is visited by the people, and the figure of Tikhon has been enshrined in the hearts of the Russian people as a martyr and saint.

NOTES

Concerning Endnotes. The notes by Jane Swan that have appeared in the original edition of this book in 1964 have been for the most part preserved, with minor corrections. Since, however, the sources which Jane Swan had at her disposal in 1964 were understandably incomplete, we saw it necessary to supplement or to correct some of information in some of these endnotes or to compose the new endnotes entirely. When these supplemental notes follow the original ones, they are separated from the latter by a pilcrow sign (¶). Additions and corrections that were done by Holy Trinity Seminary Press are marked Ed., while additional endnotes composed by Dr Scott M. Kenworthy are marked "S. M. K." at the end of the note in question.

Chapter 1

1. 200 versts is approximately 130 miles.

2. Russia, unlike Western Europe, continued to reckon by the Julian calendar. This meant a time lag of twelve days before 1900 in comparison with the Gregorian calendar, and after 1900, a time lag of thirteen days. Unless indicated, the author will date by the Gregorian calendar.

3. Vasily's father, Father Ioann Timofeevich Bellavin, was born in 1822 in the village of Sopki, where his father served as the priest. Ioann was ordained a priest in 1847 and in 1849 assigned to the Resurrection Church in the village of Klin (Toropets district, Pskov province), where he served over twenty years before

his transfer to Toropets. Vasily was born in Klin and was four years old when the family moved to Toropets in 1869. –S. M. K.

4. The history of Toropets dates back to pagan times. A large fortress is still there, rising about 42 yards high and 500 yards in circumference, whose beginnings are buried in legend. Originally the town was devoted to warlike enterprises, having battles with the Lithuanians, and as late as the seventeenth century, fighting against the Zaporozhye Cossacks in the Ukraine. Early wealth based on the silk trade had dwindled completely, until by 1870 the census revealed a population of only 5,161, all of Great Russian origin. The famous Nebin Trinity-Sergius Monastery, built in 1592, was only two miles from the town and influenced the atmosphere of the surrounding area. The town was surrounded half by forests and half by tilled land. Snow covered the land from November to April, and the lake was covered with ice all winter long. The weather was cloudy all year.

5. The priest Alexander Rozhdestvensky in his memoirs of the Patriarch entitled, *His Holiness Tikhon, Patriarch of Moscow and All Russia* (London, 1923), spoke of Tikhon's readiness to write his friends' essays for them and explain any problems of theology that they could not understand. Apparently his friends were all too ready to take advantage of Vasily's good nature.

6. The word *pechal'nik* is almost impossible to translate into English. It means a protector or caretaker, as a term for a person who looks after others with great anxiety and concern, and usually is applied to parents. This might possibly indicate that this brother would be the eldest one of the family and, after the early death of the father, may have been instrumental in the bringing up of his two younger brothers. No evidence, however, shows the respective ages of the three Bellavin brothers. ¶ Vasily Bellavin was one of four sons (not three); the others were Pavel (1857–1881), Ioann (1859–1891), and Mikhail (1873–1902); the date of his father's death has

not yet been established, but it was evidently in or around 1894. Although Swan does not cite her source for the father's prophetic dream, most versions state not that one brother will be a *pechal'nik* (someone who grieves over others), but rather an unhappy or pitiable person. Since all three of St Tikhon's brothers died relatively young, it is not clear to which brothers the dream refers. –S. M. K.

7. The four academies were in St Petersburg, Moscow, Kiev, and Kazan.

8. Perhaps nothing so reveals the character of a person as the nicknames he picks up in life. While Vasily was still at the seminary at Pskov, he was called "Bishop." This was when he was just sixteen years old, and when he later entered the Academy in St Petersburg, he was at once christened "Patriarch" by his classmates. The spiritual force within him must have been immediately clear to others from a very early age. In later years, old friends reminded Tikhon of this jocular prophetic title.

9. Even Julius Hecker, in his completely biased and highly critical book *Religion Under the Soviets* (New York: Vanguard Press, 1927), was forced to fall back on Patriarch Tikhon's happy temperament.

10. This student library was quite separate from the religious library, which belonged to the academy, and had been started by the students themselves who sold personal belongings to buy the books and periodicals.

11. Most of the students took monastic vows in their third and fourth years at the academy, and it was rare that any of them graduated while still laymen. ¶Although in earlier times academy students frequently took monastic vows as their first step on the path to becoming bishops, this was no longer the case in the St Petersburg Academy after the 1860s. –S. M. K.

12. Rozhdestvensky, *His Holiness Tikhon*, 4, tells how Tikhon's voice remained firm and clear as he spoke his vows, "Yes with God's help," and many in the church were moved with tears by the pathos of the moment.

13. The ranks of the clergy are as follows—*Black or monastic*: hierodeacon, hieromonk, igumen, archimandrite, bishop, archbishop, metropolitan, patriarch. *White or secular*: deacon, protodeacon, priest, archpriest, protopresbyter.

14. In 1595–1596, the Orthodox bishops in the Polish-Lithuanian Commonwealth (modern Ukraine and Belarus) decided to break communion with the Orthodox patriarch of Constantinople and to enter into union with the Roman Catholic Church. These bishops and those of their flock who followed them were obliged to accept the doctrines of the Church of Rome and the authority of the pope, but were allowed to retain Eastern liturgical rites. The adherents of this union are commonly called "Greek Catholics" or "Uniates."–Ed.

15. The Kholm region had been predominantly Greek Catholic (once more commonly referred to as "Uniates," though this term today is seen as condescending). Russian authorities suppressed the Greek Catholic Church in the Russian Empire over the course of the nineteenth century, and the Kholm Greek Catholic Church was the last to be dissolved in 1875. –S. M. K.

16. The following quotation is taken from Bishop Tikhon's first sermon after he was consecrated bishop of Lublin and is a good indication of his feeling about the duties and position of bishops: "In my youth, the office of a bishop seemed to me to be dignity, power, might, and honor. When I was a child I had childish conceptions. Now I know that it means work, striving, and sacrifice. It is not easy to be weak with those who are weak, nor is it easy to be an example to the faithful in word, in one's bearing, in love, faith, and chastity, and it certainly is not easy to admonish, to threaten and to punish in all patience. The life of a true bishop is daily dying in cares and concerns for others, therefore the success of the bishop's official activities depend not so much on human qualities and faculties, but much more on the power of God which is given to those who are conscious of their weakness" (Karl Rose, *Drei Patriarchen,* Berlin, c. 1950). ¶ In fact,

neither the canons, nor the pre-revolutionary church legislation established any minimal age for the consecration of a bishop, except the canonical minimum of thirty years for a presbyteral ordination. The Council of 1917–1918 was the first to set the minimal age for episcopal consecration at thirty-five years.–Ed.

17. A vicar or auxiliary bishop is a bishop who assists the ruling bishop of a larger diocese or administers part of his diocese.

18. The Diocese of Alaska and the Aleutian Islands was created in 1870, with the bishop's residence at San Francisco.

19. His brother Mikhail, who accompanied him to North America and served as his secretary and the diocesan librarian, died on November 21, 1902, in San Francisco. St Tikhon accompanied his brother's body back to Russia for burial in Toropets in 1903. –S. M. K.

20. It must be remembered that Tikhon was thrown into a completely new environment, including freedom of religion; no censorship; the hurrying, business-like American bustle; and above all a clash of Galician, Syrian, Bulgarian, Serbian, Greek, and Russian nationalities, which often must have drowned out the quiet voice of this man of God.

21. This sermon was given in December 1898, thus three years before his brother Mikhail's death. –S. M. K.

22. Rozhdestvensky, *His Holiness Tikhon*, says that Tikhon's mother died soon after he came to America but gives no date. ¶ Patriarch Tikhon's mother, Anna Gavrilovna Bellavina, passed away on April 29, 1904. In fact, she outlived three of her four sons. –Ed., S. M. K.

23. The newly established seminary had formerly been a mission school that Tikhon enlarged and changed to supply American priests for American churches and to make sure that the American churches would not depend on Russia for a constant supply of clergy. One of Tikhon's wishes was that all priests in America have American citizenship.

24. In February 1907, the first Orthodox Church Synod in America was held in Mayfield, New York. This had been

organized by Tikhon, but just a month before it met, he was transferred to Yaroslavl'.

25. In 1891, the Slovak Greek Catholic priest Alexis Toth (Tovt), with his parish community in Minneapolis, was received into the Orthodox Church, becoming part of the Diocese of Alaska and Aleutian Islands. Under his influence, from 1891 to 1909 a number of Greek Catholic parish communities and thousands of former Uniates returned to the Orthodoxy. For his missionary labours, which were supported by the future patriarch Tikhon during his tenure in North America, Fr Alexis was glorified as a saint by the Orthodox Church in America in 1994. His relics reside at St Tikhon's Monastery in South Canaan, Pa. –Ed.

26. After Mikhail's death, St Tikhon submitted a request for a three-month leave in order to return to Russia (in part to bury Mikhail in Toropets). The leave was granted in March 1903 and he departed New York on May 15/28, 1903, arriving in Toropets at the end of May. Coming to St Petersburg in mid-June, St Tikhon was called to attend the sessions of the Holy Synod, which he did until the end of the year. After celebrating Christmas in Toropets, he departed for America, arriving in New York on January 3/16, 1904. –S. M. K.

27. Russian churches traditionally have the bell tower quite separate from the main part of the church, and this tower is often the proudest piece of architecture in the town, much like the Giotto tower in Florence.

28. There is a difference between Emhardt, *Religion in Soviet Russia* (London, 1929), and Ivan Andreyev, Краткій обзоръ исторіи Русской Церкви отъ революціи до нашихъ дней [A Short History of the Russian Church from the Revolution to Our Times] (Jordanville: Holy Trinity Monastery, 1952); because several of Emhardt's dates have proved wrong, I have used Andreyev's dates here. ¶ Archbishop Tikhon was transferred to Vilnius on December 22, 1913 and arrived in Vilnius on January 24, 1914. –Ed., S. M. K.

29. Vladimir L'vov's reference to the "will of God" when speaking of the revolution is most interesting in light of Tikhon's later speeches; Tikhon also saw the chaotic state of revolution and civil strife as the will of God brought on by the materialistic attitude and indifference of the Russian people to things of the spirit, as the real cause of the upheaval, rather than the work of political groups.

30. Bishop Joasaph had been appointed by the Synod to Moscow before the new ruling on elections had been made. ¶Joasaph was appointed bishop of Dmitrovsk, one of the vicar bishops of the Moscow diocese, and temporary administrator of the diocese until a new metropolitan was elected. –S. M. K.

31. In a preliminary straw vote, Alexander D. Samarin, the former chief procurator of the Holy Synod in 1915, received most of the votes, and Tikhon was not even in the first rank of candidates. ¶ In fact, Samarin and Archbishop Tikhon received an equal share of votes in the first round of election for Metropolitan of Moscow. –Ed.

Chapter 2

1. Working from the statistics of John S. Curtiss, *The Russian Church and the Soviet State* (Boston, 1953); Matthew Spinka, *The Church and the Russian Revolution* (New York, 1927); Serge Bolshakoff, *The Christian Church and the Soviet State* (New York, 1942); and Nicholas Zernov, *The Russians and Their Church* (New York, 1945), the following breakdown can be given, as is shown in the table. ¶ These data were verified and corrected against the list of the Council members as shown in the first issue of the Conciliar Acts: The Sacred Council of the Orthodox Church of Russia, Деянія [Acts], vol. 1, issue 1 (Moscow: Publication of the Executive Committee of the Council, 1918), 119–133. –Ed.

2. This was an obvious reference to St Hermogen's heroic activities.

3. One of the peasant representatives at the council made the following statement, "We have no longer a tsar—a father whom we could love. It is impossible to love the synod, therefore we peasants wish to have a patriarch." Michael Polsky, *Новые Мученики Россійскіе* [*New Martyrs of Russia*] (Jordanville, NY, 1949), 90.

4. In fact the restoration of the patriarchate was an extremely contentious issue that was intensely debated, with the debate centering on whether the patriarchate contradicted the principle of *sobornost'*. The question became more urgent after the Bolshevik seizure of power. –S. M. K.

5. Thomas Whittemore, "The Rebirth of Religion in Russia," *National Geographic* 34 (1918): 378–401, published an eye-witness account of the destruction of the Kremlin by the fratricidal war between the Bolsheviks and the cadets. He visited the scene a few days after the Kremlin fell and gave a graphic description of the Austrian, German, Latvian, and Russian Bolshevik soldiers who were lounging about, writing obscene remarks on the wall, and either looting or wantonly destroying whatever struck their fancy. Enormous pools of blood were still to be traced by the stains and foot tracks through them. A shell had struck the central dome of the five domes of the Dormition Cathedral, leaving gaping holes and ruining centuries-old frescoes. All window glass was gone, and the altar and sanctuary were filled with debris of glass, bricks, and dirt. The Chudov Monastery was punctured with great shell-holes, relics were scattered, and precious icons were destroyed. The Church of St Nicholas, containing relics honored by all Christendom, was particularly defiled by filthy writings in both Russian and German, and the place where once the relics had been kept was turned into an outhouse. The porch of the Annunciation Cathedral, where Ivan IV admired the comet, was shot off. The cathedral of the Archangel Michael, the church of the Deposition of the Robe, the chapel of the icon of the Theotokos of the

Caves, and the church of the Forerunner all fell beneath the cannonading. The patriarchal sacristy was turned into a rubbish heap with all the ancient treasures. A book of the Holy Gospels of 1115 was ruined; miters, crosses, vessels, and church utensils of former patriarchs were all destroyed; and ruthless looters were acting as scavengers among the ruins. Church after church was either partially or completely ruined, and the orgy of chaos was completed by the unchecked pillaging.

6. A *krestniy khod* is a religious procession outside or around the church headed by clerics carrying banners and crosses, usually in honor of some religious object or event.

7. Archbishop Antony (Khrapovitsky; 1863–1936), later metropolitan and first hierarch of the Russian Church Abroad, was one of the most brilliant and well-educated churchmen of his day.

8. On the first round of elections, on October 30, it was Archbishop Kirill (Smirnov) of Tambov who received the second highest number of votes (27). On the following day, during the second round of voting, members were instructed to write three names on their ballots, and only the name that received an absolute majority could be considered a candidate. On the third round, members were instructed to write only two names and could not vote for Archbishop Antony, since he was already a candidate. –S. M. K.

9. The Vladimir Icon of the Virgin was brought to Russia from Constantinople no later than the second quarter of the twelfth century. In 1155, it was removed to the Suzdal lands from Kiev and, in 1161, placed in the Dormition Cathedral in Vladimir. In 1395, it was transferred to Moscow, to the Dormition Cathedral, and taken annually in four cross-processions. During the siege of 1812, the icon was transferred to Vladimir and Murom but returned when Napoleon retreated. From the earliest times, repeated and documented miracles have been caused by the presence of the icon, until it

became the most holy object of all Russia and the icon most venerated by the people.

10. Metropolitan Evlogy, Путь моей жизни (Paris, 1947), spoke of the extreme difficulty that the churchmen had moving the icon from the Dormition Cathedral to Christ the Saviour Cathedral.

11. Metropolitan Vladimir of Kiev was chairman of the council before Tikhon was elected as president. On February 7, 1918, he was brutally abducted from the Monastery of the Caves in Kiev and murdered by a small band of assassins.

12. *Staretz* is a saintly monk who has achieved such spiritual growth that he is expressly able to teach others.

13. Alexis (Soloviev) was a monk of the Zosimov monastery, a monastery of the strictest rule whose members lived in solitude and under vows of silence. Alexis had been a member of the preconciliar committee.

14. *Axios* is the Greek word meaning "he is worthy."

15. Related by Metropolitan Evlogy in Путь моей жизни.

16. Polsky, Новые Мученики Российскіе [*New Martyrs of Russia*], 91 (translated by the writer).

17. After the installation ceremony, telegrams poured in from across Russia, congratulating both the new patriarch and the council. Curtiss, *The Russian Church and the Soviet State*, 39.

18. The kukol is a white-rounded headdress worn by the patriarch.

19. All during the ceremony of enthronement, the patriarchal throne was next to the empty throne of the tsar.

20. Whenever a bishop gives a sermon, he is handed his staff, which he holds during the actual speech.

21. Ivan the Great is the most famous bell tower in Moscow.

22. Polsky, Новые Мученики Российскіе [*New Martyrs of Russia*], 92–93.

23. Polsky, Ibid., 93.

24. Evlogy, Путь моей жизни; Polsky, Новые Мученики Россійскіе [*New Martyrs of Russia*]; Rozhdestvensky, *His Holiness Tikhon*; Metropolitan Anastassy, Памяти Святѣйшаго Патріарха Тихона [In memory of the Most Holy Patriarch Tikhon] (Jordanville, NY, 1950).

25. Archbishop Anastassy (Gribanovsky) of Kishinev and Khotin strongly supported the revival of the patriarchate. In 1936 he became the first hierarch of the Russian Church Abroad. ¶ Metropolitan Anastassy retired in 1964 and reposed next year. – Ed.

26. Metropolitan Agathangel of Yaroslavl' was one of Tikhon's most trusted supporters and later was designated as Tikhon's deputy in 1922.

27. Anastassy, Памяти Святѣйшаго Патріарха Тихона [In Memory of the Most Holy Patriarch Tikhon], 21, footnote.

28. This story was recorded by Metropolitan Evlogy, Путь моей жизни, from actual experience, for Evlogy had been a teacher at the Kholm Seminary when Tikhon was rector.

29. "Лѣтопись Россіи: московскіе воспоминанія 1923–1927," *Лѣтопись: органъ православной культуры* 1 (1937): 64, 65.

30. The physical description of Patriarch Tikhon was given to the present writer by Metropolitan Anastassy who knew him well.

Chapter 3

1. The patriarch's duties as diocesan bishop of Moscow were delegated in fact to the patriarch's vicar bishop who had the title of Archbishop of Kolomna and Mozhaysk.

2. Stavropigial monasteries were those monasteries directly subject to the jurisdiction of the supreme church administration.

3. Spinka, *The Church and the Russian Revolution*, 96–97.

4. Ibid., 102.

5. Ibid., 103.

6. Ibid., 103.

7. Ibid., 104.

8. Ibid., 104.

9. Ibid., 105–6.

10. For a detailed picture of the position of the church after the Revolution, see Vladimir Gsovski, "The Legal Status of the Church in Soviet Russia," *Fordham Law Review* 8.1 (1939): 1–28. ¶ The preceding two paragraphs describe the legal status of the Russian Orthodox Church during the Soviet period, as of 1964, when this book was originally published. The legal status of the Church has radically changed after the fall of the Soviet Union, and thus, this information is largely obsolete. –Ed.

11. Ibid., 18–19.

12. Decree of 23 January 1918, art. 9.

13. The first attempt to carry out the December 4 decree of nationalization of property was at St Alexander Nevsky Lavra in Petrograd. A government official was sent to demand the surrender of all cash and other assets to the Commissariat of Welfare. The head of the monastery refused to comply, and at a meeting, the entire monastic community voted not to surrender any part of the property and to oppose any attempt on the part of the government to disperse them.

14. Spinka, *The Church and the Russian Revolution*, 118–22. ¶ Here and further the translations originally taken by the author from Matthew Spinka's book have been verified and corrected against the original Russian text. –Ed.

15. Ibid, 122.

16. Ibid, 122.

17. Resolution of the Most Holy Patriarch Tikhon and the Holy Synod, "On the Activity of the Church Administration under the Conditions of the New State Power" (February 28, 1918), in M.E. Gubonin, ed. Акты Святейшего Тихона, патриарха Московского и всея России [The Acts of the Most Holy Tikhon, Patriarch of Moscow and All Russia] (Moscow: St Tikhon's Orthodox Institute, 1994), 96–98. –Ed.

18. Kirill Zaitsev, Православная Церковь въ Совѣтской Россіи [The Orthodox Church in Soviet Russia] (Shanghai, 1945), 31.

19. Ibid., 35.

20. Konstantin Rozov (1874–1923) was the most famous deacon of his time because of his magnificent voice. He often was referred to as the Chaliapin of the church.

21. A series of pictures depicting the damage done to the Kremlin by the Bolsheviks, pictures of the council, and pictures of Patriarch Tikhon during his trip to Petrograd are described by Thomas Whittemore, "The Rebirth of Religion in Russia," *National Geographic* 34 (1918): 378–401.

22. A panikhida is a prayer service for the departed.

23. In a conversation with the author, Metropolitan Anastassy claims that Tikhon actually called the murders regicides as well as all those who aided or sympathized with them.

24. Zaitsev, Православная Церковь въ Совѣтской Россіи [The Orthodox Church in Soviet Russia], 25.

25. The Dormition fast in honor of the Feast of the Dormition of the Theotokos is one of the four fasts in the Orthodox Church year calendar. It lasts from August 1 to 15 on the Julian calendar.

26. Zaitsev, Православная Церковь въ Совѣтской Россіи [The Orthodox Church in Soviet Russia], 41–43.

27. Spinka, *The Church and the Russian Revolution*, 142.

28. Ibid., 145.

29. When the Provisional Government granted the coming council the right to work out a new form of church government at its coming assemblage, it also had granted one million rubles for its expenses. No further grant was ever made either by the provisional government or the Soviet government.

30. The 1918 constitution of the Russian Socialist Federal Soviet Republic also deprived all monks and priests of any

denomination the right to vote. Andre Rothstein, ed., *The Soviet Constitution* (London, 1923).

31. Emhardt, *Religion in Soviet Russia*, 29–30.

32. Bolshakoff, *The Christian Church and the Soviet State*, 35.

33. Vladimir Lenin, *Religion*, Little Lenin Library (New York, 1935), vii, 16.

34. Zaitsev, Православная Церковь въ Совѣтской Россіи [The Orthodox Church in Soviet Russia], 43–46.

35. Polsky, Новые Мученики Россійскіе [New Martyrs of Russia], 100.

36. Paul B. Anderson, *People, Church and State in Modern Russia* (New York, 1944), 63, reported this case from a worker's journal called *Godless at the Workbench*.

37. Zaitsev, Православная Церковь въ Совѣтской Россіи [The Orthodox Church in Soviet Russia], 78.

38. Ibid., 82.

39. Polsky, Новые Мученики Россійскіе [New Martyrs of Russia], 97.

40. Kasha is a dish made out of buckwheat, which resembles brown rice when it is cooked.

41. Shchi is cabbage soup.

Chapter 4

1. Spinka, *The Church and the Russian Revolution*, 162.

2. Ibid., 163.

3. A. A. Valentinov, *The Black Book* (Paris, 1925), 158.

4. Spinka, *The Church and the Russian Revolution*, 168, gives this quotation taken from a speech of Krasikov at the trial of Metropolitan Veniamin in *Revolution and the Church* 1–3 (1923), 83.

5. Ibid., 168.

6. Pomgol is the abbreviation for the Central Committee for Aid of the Starving.

7. Spinka, *The Church and the Russian Revolution*, gives some of the actual pleas taken from issues of *Izvestia*.

8. *Izvestia*, no. 46, February 26, 1922.

9. Valentinov, *The Black Book*, 253–4, appendix I.

10. That the confiscation of the church treasures was more an attack on the church than a method of aiding the starving was shown by repeated attempts of the people to offer the value of the consecrated objects in rubles to the government officials, only to be refused in every case.

11. Emhardt, *Religion in Soviet Russia*, 48–49, quotes several of these cases based on records taken from the official newspapers *Pravda* and *Izvestia*.

12. *Izvestia*, no. 90, April 26, 1922 and no. 99, May 6, 1922.

13. Curtiss, *The Russian Church and the Soviet State*, 120, quotes this from *Izvestia*, no. 99, May 6, 1922.

14. In the spring of 1921, Patriarch Tikhon had appointed Archbishop Evlogy head of the Russian church in Western Europe. ¶ The decree was issued by Patriarch Tikhon on April 8, 1921. –Ed.

15. The message of Patriarch Tikhon in November 17, 1921, against ritual innovations and those who were trying to change the church's liturgical traditions should have forced Vvedensky out of the Orthodox Church at that point, for he was one of the worst offenders on these scores, but Metropolitan Veniamin personally interceded and protected him at the time.

16. Curtiss, *The Russian Church and the Soviet State*, 125.

17. I. Brikhnichev, Патриарх Тихон и его церковь [Patriarch Tikhon and His Church] (Moscow, 1923), 19–20.

18. Bishop Antonin's role in the revolution of 1905 was so detrimental to church prestige and challenging to Synod authority that he was retired. From then on he refused to mention the tsar's name in the liturgy. He was a witness for the government against the fifty-four and even accepted the Soviet invitation to be a member of Pomgol. He was one of the original members of the Living Church movement but later split with them to form his own dissenting group.

19. Curtiss, *The Russian Church and the Soviet State.*

20. Zaitsev, Православная Церковь въ Совѣтской Россіи [The Orthodox Church in Soviet Russia], 103.

21. Spinka, *The Church and the Russian Revolution*, 192–4.

22. *Izvestia*, March 30, 1922.

23. Quoted from *Izvestia*, no. 106, May 14, 1922, in Spinka, *The Church and the Russian Revolution*, 196–8.

24. The death penalty was carried out in only five cases, and the reprieved six were given extended prison terms. This, however, was unknown to the patriarch during the two interviews with Vvedensky and his colleagues.

25. A. A. Vvedensky, *The Church and the Government* (Moscow, 1923), 110.

26. Captain Francis McCullagh, who knew most of the high church men including Patriarch Tikhon and had frequent talks with them, in his *The Bolshevik Persecution of Christianity* (London, 1924), 38–40, claims that on May 12 the liberal priests got the patriarch out of bed to demand that he appoint Bishop Antonin as his successor. It is not clear whether this was a second visit made on May 12 or was the beginning of the long talk between the delegation and the patriarch.

27. Spinka, *The Church and the Russian Revolution*, 201–2.

28. Quoted from *The Messenger*, no. 2, 1925, 18, the official organ of the Holy Synod, by Spinka, *The Church and the Russian Revolution*, 201.

29. Quoted from *The Messenger*, no. 2, 1925, 18, by Spinka, *The Church and the Russian Revolution*, 202–3.

30. Emhardt, *Religion in Soviet Russia*, 63.

31. Spinka, *The Church and the Russian Revolution*, 213–15.

32. Without waiting for the imminent council of the Living Church, the conference took on itself the authority to appoint Archpriest John Albinsky, a married man, as a bishop, thus carrying out the revolt of the White clergy against the Black clergy.

33. *The Living Church*, no. 8–9, 1922, 8.

34. Krasnitsky himself told of a visit to Kalinin asking for government aid in gaining control of the Cathedral of Christ the Saviour in Moscow. Kalinin had the contract with the parish canceled and a new one drawn up to the Living Church members. At the same time, Krasnitsky assured Kalinin that the bishops who were fighting the Living Church were all counterrevolutionaries and requested a ban on church congresses without the permission of the central authorities of the Living Church to prevent counterrevolutionary elements from holding local church gatherings. All this was granted by Kalinin. Curtiss, *The Russian Church and the Soviet State*, 141.

35. Boris Titlinov, Новая Церковь [The New Church] (Petrograd, 1923), 17–20.

36. The hostility displayed by the people to the Living Church was so strong that the priests often dared not go on the streets. Vvedensky, himself, was stoned, and although the Living Church at one time controlled most church buildings, the services were almost unattended. Many of the original supporters of the reform group, such as Metropolitan Sergius of Vladimir, quickly recanted.

37. See Chapter 3.

38. By election, the Supreme Ecclesiastical Administration consisted of five bishops, twelve priests, one deacon, and two laymen. The Central Executive Committee of the Living Church was composed of twenty-five members.

39. "Many Years" is a hymn customarily sung in the Orthodox Church in honor of some feted person wishing many more years of life and prosperity.

40. *Acts of the Second All-Russian Local Sobor of the Orthodox Church* (Moscow), May 2, 1923, 6.

41. For a complete description of the Living Church, the essay *Religion in Soviet Russia* was prepared by Sergius Troitsky, master of theology in Kiev, and William Chancey Emhardt, head of the Slavic Division of Columbia University,

with an introduction by Clarence Manning of the Slavic Division of Columbia University (London, 1929). A remnant of this movement existed until 1946 when the new patriarch Alexis, who was elected with Stalin's permission, received it back into the patriarchal Church.

42. *Acts of the Second All-Russian Local Sobor of the Orthodox Church,* op. cit. pp. 6–8.

Chapter 5

1. *Izvestia*, no. 76, April 6, 1923.

2. Zaitsev, Православная Церковь въ Совѣтской Россіи [The Orthodox Church in Soviet Russia], gives numerous quotations from the *Times* (London), showing the ferocity of the attack on the Communists conducted in England. Apparently, all sections of public opinion were vitally interested in what was happening.

3. Lord Curzon had for a long time been upset by Lloyd George's flirtation with Russia and by the Anglo-Russian trade agreement concluded in March 1921. After the Treaty of Rapallo following the Genoa Conference, he felt that Russia should be stopped. The 1923 Cieplak–Budkevich affair, in which two Polish Roman Catholic clergymen were arrested by NKVD and one—Konstantin Budkevich—executed, drew a sharp protest from the British government only to be answered by a note from the Soviet Foreign Minister Chicherin speaking of the Irish atrocities. At this point, Curzon, drawing his evidence chiefly from intelligence reports, a most undiplomatic procedure, sent back a long protest citing incident after incident and demanding that Russia back down completely in her insulting inferences and refrain from challenging notes. The case of Patriarch Tikhon was cited in this British ultimatum.

4. Translated by Curtiss, *The Russian Church and the Soviet State,* 159–60.

5. *Izvestia*, no. 142, June 28, 1923.

6. Emhardt, *Religion in Soviet Russia*, 133, quotes this account but does not give his source for fear of harming his informant. He credits the story and apparently completely trusted the person who related it to him.

7. Zaitsev, Православная Церковь въ Совѣтской Россіи [The Orthodox Church in Soviet Russia], 141–2.

8. In May 1919, Leonid Krasin was sent to England as the head of the Russian Trade Delegation and stayed on as an unofficial representative of the Soviet Government.

9. Spinka, *The Church and the Russian Revolution*, 253, cites this cartoon from a paper in Moscow called *The Work-man's Moscow*, July 15, 1923.

10. Zaitsev, Православная Церковь въ Совѣтской Россіи [The Orthodox Church in Soviet Russia], 148–49.

11. Polsky, Новые Мученики Россійскіе [New Martyrs of Russia], 123.

12. *Guardian* (Manchester), July 15, 1923.

13. As soon as Tikhon returned to the Donskoy Monastery, he was interviewed by a Soviet reporter, and according to the article printed in *Izvestia*, no. 143, June 1923, he declared that he had been well treated in prison and had not suffered torture. His appearance on the day he was released did not support this statement. He also was said to have declared that he had broken with the counter-revolution and stood completely outside of politics. He declared he did not consider himself deposed by the Renovationists and would at once resume his ecclesiastical duties.

14. A moleben is a short service for a special occasion.

15. Reprinted in the *American Orthodox Messenger*, no. 13, July 30, 1923, translated by Spinka, *The Church and the Russian Revolution*, 255–60.

16. Polsky, Новые Мученики Россійскіе [New Martyrs of Russia], 105.

17. A strange incident occurred in 1923–24 at Constantinople showing the complete lack of understanding of church

affairs in Russia outside of the country. This misunderstanding still exists in many respects. Patriarch Meletius IV of Constantinople originally had condemned the deposition of Tikhon and the second council on July 4, 1923, but soon afterward died. His successor, Patriarch Gregory VII, rescinded this decision, and on the basis of loyalty to the new government decided to appoint an investigation committee to go to Russia, recognize the loyal group, and ostracize the disloyal group. He also advised the Russian patriarch to resign immediately and stated that the whole patriarchate in Russia should be abolished. This was in May 1924. The following answer to Gregory's advice was given by Tikhon and was published in the *Ecclesiastical Journal of Karlovtsy* (Yugoslavia), nos. 7 and 8 (1925):

> Having perused the above-mentioned protocols, we were not a little saddened, as well as amazed, that the representative of the Ecumenical Patriarchate, the head of the Constantinopolitan church, without any preparatory correspondence with us, as the lawful representative and head of the whole Russian church, should intrude himself into the life and affairs of the autocephalous Russian church. The holy Councils (cf. canons 2 and 3 of the II Ecumenical Council, and others), ever acknowledged in the past as well as now, that the Constantinopolitan bishop possesses a preeminence of honor above other autocephalous churches, but not of authority. We also recall that canon which specifies that "when not invited, bishops must not go outside the limits of their territory to consecrate another, or for any other ecclesiastical function." Hence any attempt of any commission whatsoever without reference to me, as the sole legal and orthodox primate of the Russian Orthodox Church, is illegal, without my authorization, and will not be received by the Orthodox Russian people, and will result not in pacification, but in a still greater disturbance

and schism in the life of the already heavily afflicted Russian Orthodox Church. In the end, it will be beneficial only to our schismatically new churchmen, whose leaders now at the head of the so-called Holy Synod, as the former archbishop of Nizhny Novgorod, Evdokim and others, are deprived by me of their priestly office and "till further disposition," on account of the disturbance, schism, and illegal seizure of ecclesiastical government which they effected, are pronounced to be outside the fellowship of the Orthodox Church.

In spite of this, the commission came and pronounced in favor of the Synodal party and sent an accredited representative there. Following suit, all the other patriarchs sided with the Living Church with the exception of Gregory of Antioch and Demetrius of Serbia.

18. News of the public repentance in Moscow soon seeped down into the villages, although the Living Church priests tried to keep the parishioners from finding out. At once many of the villages demanded to return to the patriarch's jurisdiction and if the priest proved recalcitrant, the people in a crowd went to the nearest town to learn the facts and on more than one occasion returned with a new "Batiushka," the endearing form for a priest that means "little father."

19. Certain high dignitaries who went through the grueling ordeal of public repentance were Bishop Artemy (Ilyinsky), head of the Renovationist church in Petrograd, Archbishop Konstantin (Bulychev) of Mogilev, Archbishop Serafim (Meshcheryakov) of Kostroma, and most important, Metropolitan Sergius (Stragorodsky) of Vladimir.

20. The patriarch was influenced by the fact that many of the working men were unable to attend church on the holidays because of the difference between the two calendars and because they were fined if they missed work. This complaint

had been given to Tikhon several times in the form of petitions. It was not until the late 1930s that some of the biggest church holidays were moved to the rest days of the official Soviet week without changing the church calendar.

21. Polsky, Новые Мученики Россійскіе [New Martyrs of Russia], 108–9.

22. Actually at one point the GPU agent induced Tikhon to remove an anti-Soviet bishop, but as soon as the agent left and Tikhon recovered his composure, he promptly reinstated him.

23. It was precisely this document that Peter of Krutitsy, the patriarch's successor, refused to sign, which sent him to Siberia and which Metropolitan Sergius finally agreed to in July 1927.

24. Although Tikhon was released from prison, he was never cleared of his charges, nor convicted. He remained in a sense outside of the law in the eyes of the government, the defrocked citizen Bellavin. Queries to the government from various parishes about prayers for Patriarch Tikhon received the answer that prayers in the service for the patriarch were illegal and might be punished by the loss of the church contract, if there was the slightest demonstration of feelings.

25. *Izvestia*, no. 67, March 22, 1924.

26. It was precisely these scientifically minded peasants and workers who flocked to the churches to celebrate thanksgiving molebens when news of the cancellation of the case against the patriarch became public.

27. *Izvestia*, no. 67, March 22, 1924.

28. It is the Russian Orthodox custom to celebrate one's namesday, that is the day that the church celebrates the saint's day whom one is named for, rather than one's own birthday.

29. This deputation from America must have given Tikhon particular pleasure, for the courts in the state of New York had just upheld the legal claims of an appointee of the Holy Synod (Living Church) as Archbishop of North

America, who later was to gain possession of the property of St Nicholas Cathedral of New York founded by Tikhon.

30. Polsky, Новые Мученики Россійскіе [New Martyrs of Russia], 105–6.

31. It was precisely at this time that Krasnitsky was negotiating with Tikhon and eventually returned for a short while to the Patriarchal Church. It was hoped that the breach would be healed by his defection, but his return was just another maneuver with no purpose.

32. A lampada is an oil lamp that is kept burning in front of an icon.

33. Ivan M. Andreyev, "О Положеніи Православной Церкви въ Совѣтском Союзѣ" [On the Status of the Russian Orthodox Church in the Soviet Union], 6.

34. After many vicissitudes on the part of the churchmen, Metropolitan Sergius organized the Temporary Patriarchal Synod in May 1927 and succeeded in having NKVD recognize it as a legal central administration. This move, while giving a certain legal position to the church, put it directly under the control of the government and fulfilled the fears of the dying Patriarch Tikhon.

35. Polsky, Новые Мученики Россійскіе [New Martyrs of Russia], 119.

36. Ibid., 117.

37. Ibid., 119–22.

38. The dikery and trikery are candlesticks used by the bishop during liturgical services to bless the people.

39. The burial of Patriarch Tikhon took place on Palm Sunday, 1925, and for this reason, in his funeral speech Bishop Boris (Rukin) of Mozhaysk called on the people to sing "Hosanna, blessed is He that cometh in the name of the Lord" before the coffin of the patriarch. It is more customary to sing "Eternal Memory" or "Holy God" at the conclusion of an Orthodox funeral service. –Ed.

Chapter 6

1. *Izvestia*, no. 86, April 15, 1925.

2. Ibid.

3. Curtiss, *The Russian Church and the Soviet State*, 175–6, quotes a statement made to Matthew Spinka by Petr G. Smidovich who was in charge of the party secretariate for the affairs of the cults. In a personal interview with Spinka, he said that the patriarch, whom he originally distrusted, had turned out to be an honorable man who kept his promises, but seemed to be very weak and easily influenced by those around him.

4. Andreyev's *Short History of the Russian Church from the Revolution to Our Time* deals with all church documents upon which he has spent his life in a detailed study. He devotes a very short section to the will, but a very definite and clear opinion is given, backed up with undisputable proof.

BIBLIOGRAPHY

Akhmatov, Ivan. *Атласъ географическій, историческій и хронологическій Россійскаго государства* [Geographical, historical, and chronological atlas of the State of Russia]. St Petersburg: Einerling, 1845.

Anastassy (Gribanovsky), Metropolitan. "Святѣйшій Патріархъ Тихонъ, характеръ его личности и дѣятельности" [The Most Holy Patriarch Tikhon, the Nature of His Personality and Work]. In *Памяти Свят ѣйшаго Патріарха Тихона: к двадцатипятилѣтию со дня кончины (25 марта/7 апреля 1925–25 марта/7 апреля 1950 г. P. 16–39.* Jordanville: Holy Trinity Monastery, 1950.

Anderson, Paul B. *People, Church and State in Modern Russia.* New York: Macmillan, 1944.

Andreyev, Ivan M. *Святѣйшій Патріархъ Тихонъ и судьбы Русской Церкви* [The Most Holy Patriarch Tikhon and the Fate of the Russian Church].

Andreyev, Ivan M. *Памяти Свят ѣйшаго Патріарха Тихона* [In Memory of The Most Holy Patriarch Tikhon]. Jordanville: Holy Trinity Monastery, 1950.

Andreyev, Ivan M. *Краткій обзоръ исторіи Русской Церкви отъ революціи до нашихъ дней* [A Brief Survey of the

History of the Russian Church from the Revolution to Our Times]. Jordanville: Holy Trinity Monastery, 1951.

Andreyev, Ivan M. "О положеніи Православной Церкви въ Совѣтскомъ Союзѣ" [On the Status of the Orthodox Church in the Soviet Union]. *Православная Русь* 1/476 (1951): 4–10.

Andreyev, Ivan M. *Заметки о катакомбной Церкви в СССР* [Notes on the Catacomb Church in the USSR]. Jordanville, 1947.

Bolshakoff, Serge. *The Christian Church and the Soviet State.* New York: Macmillan, 1942.

Brianchaninov, Nicholas. *The Russian Church.* London: Burns, Oates, and Washbourne, 1931.

Briem, Efraim. *Kommunismus und Religion in der Sowjetunion: ein Ideenkampf* [Communism and Religion in the Soviet Union. A Struggle of Ideas]. Basel: F. Reinhardt, 1948.

Brikhnichev, Iona. *Патриарх Тихон и его церковь* [Patriarch Tikhon and His Church]. Moscow, 1923.

Casey, Robert P. *Religion in Russia.* New York, London: Harper and Brothers, 1946.

Curtiss, John S. *Church and State in Russia.* New York: Octagon Books, 1940.

Curtiss, John S. *The Russian Church and the Soviet State, 1917–1950.* Boston: Little, Brown, 1953.

Dearmer, Percy et al. *The Russian Church: Lectures on Its History, Constitution, Doctrine, and Ceremonial.* Preface by the Lord Bishop of London. London: S.P.C.K., 1915.

Deutscher, Isaac. *Stalin: A Political Biography.* London, New York: Oxford University Press, 1949.

Emhardt, William C. *Religion in Soviet Russia: Anarchy.* London: Mowbray, 1929.

Evlogy (Georgievsky), Metropolitan. *Путь моей жизни* [The Path of My Life]. Paris, 1947.

Fedotov, Georgiy P. *The Russian Church Since the Revolution*. London: S.P.C.K., New York: Macmillan, 1928.

Fisher, George P. *History of the Christian Church*. New York: Scribner's Sons, 1904.

Florinsky, Michael T. *The End of the Russian Empire*. New Haven: Yale University Press, 1931.

Gsovski, Vladimir. "The Legal Status of the Church in Soviet Russia." *Fordham Law Review* 8.1(1939): 1–28.

Hecker, Julius F. *Religion Under the Soviets*. New York: Vanguard Press, 1927.

D'Herbigny, Michel. *Après la more du patriarche Tykhon: les patriarcats de Constantinople et de Moscu, projets anglo-orthodoxes de concile oecuménique Grecs et Russes en Europe et en Amérique*. Orientalia Christiana 4.2/15. Rome: Pontificio Istituto Orientale, 1925.

Ilyin, Ivan A. (S.P.) *О Церкви въ СССР* [Concerning the Church in the USSR]. Introduction by Anton V. Kartashev. Paris: Études et éditions étrangères, 1947.

Kitchin, George. *Prisoner of the O.G.P.U.* London, New York: Longmans, Green and co., 1935.

Latourette, Kenneth S. *History of Christianity*. New York: Harper, 1953.

Lenin, Vladimir I. *Religion*. New York: International Publishers, 1935.

Lieb, Fritz. *Russland unterwegs: der russische Mensch zwischen Christentum und Kommunismus*. Bern: A. Francke, 1945.

Lossky, Nicholas O. *History of Russian Philosophy*. New York: International Universities Press, 1951.

Maynard, John. *Russia in Flux: Before October*. London: Victor Gollancz, 1941.

McCullagh, Francis. *The Bolshevik Persecution of Christianity*. London: J. Murray, 1924.

Medlin, William K. *Moscow and East Rome: A Political Study of the Relations of Church and State in Muscovite Russia*. Geneve: E. Droz, 1952.

Miliukov, Pavel N. *Outlines of Russian Culture*. Vol. 1.
Philadelphia: University of Pennsylvania Press, 1942.

Nicholson, Harold. *Curzon: The Last Phase, 1919–1925:
A Study in Post-War Diplomacy*. New York: Houghton
Mifflin, 1934.

Pares, Bernard. *The Fall of the Russian Monarchy*. New York,
1939.

Pobedonostsev, Konstantin P. *Исторія Православной
Церкви до начала раздѣленія церквей* [History of
the Orthodox Church Until the Beginning of
the Schism]. St Petersburg: Izd. K. P. Pobedonostseva,
1898.

Polsky, Mikhail. *Новые Мученики Россійскіе* [New Martyrs of
Russia]. Jordanville: Holy Trinity Monastery, 1949.

Polsky, Mikhail. *Каноническое положеніе высшей церковной
власти въ СССР и заграницей* [The Canonical Status of the
Supreme Church Authority in the USSR and Abroad].
Jordanville: Holy Trinity Monastery, 1948.

Priest of the English Church, *The Holy Eastern Church: a
Popular Outline of Its History, Doctrines, Liturgies, and
Vestments*. Preface by Richard F. Littledale. 2nd ed.
London: J.T. Hayes, 1873.

Rahr, Gleb. *Плѣненная Церковь: очеркъ развитія
взаимоотношеній между Церковью и властью въ СССР*
[The Church in Captivity: Essay on the Relations Between
the Church and the State in the USSR]. Frankfurt am
Main: Posev, 1954.

Rose, Karl. *Drei Patriarchen von Moskau und ganz Rußland:
Tychon, Sergius, Alexius*. Ökumenische Profile 3.3. Berlin:
Heimatdienst-Verlag, c. 1950.

Rothstein, Andrew, ed. *The Soviet Constitution*. London:
Labour Publishing Company, 1923.

Rozhdestvensky, Alexander. *His Holiness Tikhon, Patriarch of
Moscow and of All Russia*. London: S.P.C.K., New York:
Macmillan, 1923.

Rudnev, Sergius P. *Всероссійскій Церковный Соборъ и избраніе и поставленіе Святѣйшаго Тихона, Патріарха Московскаго и всея Россіи* [The All-Russian Church Council, the Election and Enthronement of the Most Holy Tikhon, Patriarch of Moscow and all Russia]. Harbin, 1929.

Spasov, G. *Freedom of Religion in the U.S.S.R.* London: Soviet News, 1951.

Spinka, Matthew. *The Church and the Russian Revolution.* New York: Macmillan, 1927.

Swan, Jane Ballard. "A Biography of Patriarch Tikhon." Doctoral dissertation. University of Pennsylvania, 1955.

Timasheff, Nicholas S. *Religion in Soviet Russia: 1917–1942.* New York: Sheed and Ward, 1942.

Titlinov, Boris V. *Новая Церковь* [The New Church]. Petrograd: Petrograd, 1923.

Valentinov, Alexander A. *Черная Книга* [The Black Book]. Paris: Russian National Student Union, 1925.

Vvedensky, Alexander A. *Церковь и Государство* [The Church and the State]. Moscow, 1923.

Vyshinsky, Andrey Ya. *The Law of the Soviet State.* New York: Macmillan, 1948.

Whittemore, Thomas. "The Rebirth of Religion in Russia." *National Geographic* 34 (1918): 378–401.

(Zaitsev), Archimandrite Konstantin (Kirill). *Православная Церковь въ Совѣтской Россіи* [The Orthodox Church in Soviet Russia]. Shanghai, 1947.

(Zaitsev), Archimandrite Konstantin (Kirill) *Памяти послѣдняго Патріарха* [In Memory of the Last Patriarch]. Jordanville: Holy Trinity Monastery, 1949.

(Zaitsev), Archimandrite Konstantin (Kirill) "Патріархъ Тихонъ – Ангелъ Русской Православной Церкви." [Patriarch Tikhon: Angel of the Russian Orthodox Church]. *Православный Путь* (1950): 38–54.

Zernov, Nicholas. *The Russians and Their Church.* New York: Macmillan, 1945.

Bibliography of Publications on St Tikhon of Moscow[*]

(A) Sources

Gubonin, M. E. (ed.). *Акты Святейшего Тихона, Патриарха Московского и всея России, позднейшие документы и переписка о каноническом преемстве высшей церковной власти, 1917–1943.* Moscow: St Tikhon's Theological Institute, 1994.

Gubonin, M. E. (ed). *Современники о патриархе Тихоне,* 2 vols. Moscow: PSTGU, 2007.

Krivosheeva, N. A. (ed). *"В годину гнева Божия…": Послания, слова и речи св. Патриарха Тихона.* Moscow: PSTGU, 2009.

Krivosheeva, N. A. (ed). *"Приспело время подвига…": Документы священного Собора Православной Российской Церкви 1917–1918 гг. о начале гонений на Церковь.* Moscow: PSTGU, 2012.

Pokrovskii, N. N. and S. G. Petrov (eds.). *Архивы Кремля: Политбюро и церковь, 1922–1925,* 2 vols. Moscow: ROSSPEN, 1997–1998.

Popov, A. V. (ed). *Американский период жизни и деятельности святителя Тихона Московского, 1898–1907 гг.* St Petersburg: Satis, 2013.

Popov, A. V. (ed). *Американский период жизни и деятельности святителя Тихона Московского: проповеди, статьи.* St Petersburg: Satis, 2011.

Popov, A. V. (ed). *Американский период жизни и деятельности святителя Тихона Московского: Письма святителя Тихона.* St Petersburg: Satis, 2010.

Regel'son, Lev. *Трагедия Русской Церкви, 1917–1945.* Paris: YMCA-Press, 1977; Moscow: Krutitskoe podvor'e, 1996.

Schulz, Günther (ed). *Священный Собор Православной Российской Церкви 1917–1918 гг.: Обзор деяний,* 3 vols. Moscow: Izd. Krutitskogo podvor'ia, 2000–2002.

[*] Compiled by Scott M. Kenworthy.

Solov'ev, E. V. *Святейший Патриарх Московский и всея России Тихон в воспоминаниях современников.* Moscow: Krutitskoe podvor'e, 2000.

Stricker, Gerd (ed). *Русская Православная Церковь в советское время (1917–1991): Материалы и документы по истории отношений между государством и Церковью,* 2 vols. Moscow: Propilei, 1995.

Vorob'ev, Vladimir (ed). *Следственное дело Патриарха Тихона: сборник документов.* Moscow: PSTGU, 2000.

(B) STUDIES

Desvitelle, Hyacinthe. *The Moscow Council (1917–1918): The Creation of Conciliar Institutions of the Russian Orthodox Church,* ed. Michael Plekon and Vitaly Permiakov, trans. Jerry Ryan. Notre Dame, IN: University of Notre Dame Press, 2014.

Efimov, A. B. and Lasaeva, O. V. *Алеутская и Северо-Американская епархия при святителе Тихоне.* Moscow: PSTGU, 2012.

Evtuhov, Catherine. "The Church in the Russian Revolution: Arguments for and against Restoring the Patriarchate at the Church Council of 1917–1918," *Slavic Review* 50 (1991): 497–511.

Kenworthy, Scott M. *The Heart of Russia: Trinity-Sergius, Monasticism and Society after 1825.* New York: Oxford University Press, 2010.

Kenworthy, Scott M. "Russian Reformation? The Program for Religious Renovation in the Orthodox Church, 1922–1925," *Modern Greek Studies Yearbook* 16/17 (2000–01): 89–130.

Kishkovsky, Leonid. "Archbishop Tikhon in America," *St Vladimir's Theological Quarterly* 19: 1 (1975): 9–31.

Krivova, N. A. "The Events in Shuia: A Turning Point in the Assault on the Church," *Russian Studies in History* 46: 2 (2007): 8–38.

Lobanov, V. V. *Патриарх Тихон и Советская власть (1917–1925 гг.)*. Moscow: Panorama, 2008.

Markova, A. A. *Святитель Тихон, Патриарх Московский и всея России*. Moscow: Blagovest, 2011.

Odintsov, M. I. *Русские Патриархи XX века: судьбы отечества и Церкви на страницах архивных документов*. Moscow: RAGS, 1999.

Roslof, Edward E. "Russian Orthodoxy and the Tragic Fate of Patriarch Tikhon (Bellavin)," in *The Human Tradition in Modern Russia*, ed. William B. Husband (Wilmington, DE: SR Books, 2000), 77–91.

Roslof, Edward E. *Red Priests: Renovationism, Russian Orthodoxy, and Revolution, 1905–1946*. Bloomington, IN: Indiana University Press, 2002.

Safonov, Dimitrii. *Святитель Тихон, Патриарх Московский и всея России и его время*. Moscow: Pokrov Foundation, 2013.

Shirokov, Sergii. *Святитель Тихон, Патриарх Московский, просветитель Северной Америки: миссионерское служение и духовное наследие*. Moscow: Center for Missionary Studies, 2009.

Tikhon (Zatekin). *Святитель Тихон, Патриарх Московский и всея России*, 2 vols. Nizhny Novgorod: Nizhny Novgorod Diocese Publications Department, 2010–2011.

Vorob'ev, Vladimir (ed). *1917-й: Церковь и судьбы России. К 90-летию Поместного Собора и избрания Патриарха Тихона*. Moscow: PSTGU, 2008.

Vostryshev, Mikhail. *Патриарх Тихон*, 4th ed. Moscow: Molodaia Gvardiia, 2009.

INDEX

Citations in parentheses following page numbers refer to note numbers; for example, p. 52(n1) refers to the text associated with note 1 on page 52.

as archbishop of Vilnius, 6,
123(n28)
as bishop of Aleutian Islands/
Alaska, 2, 4, 122(n18)
as bishop of Lublin, 4,
121–22(n16)
as librarian, 3, 120(n10)
as rector of Kazan Seminary,
3
arrest of, 88
arrest threatened of, 52
attempted murder of, 53, 99
Brest Litovsk peace and,
39–40, 43
birth of, 1, 116, 119(n3)
British press and, 84, 135(n3)
brothers of, 1–2, 119–20(n6),
122(n19), 123(n26)
burial service of, 106,
140–41(n39)
calendar change and, 97,
139(n20)
challenges by revolutionary
leaders to, 69, 71
character traits of, 19–21,
115–16, 120(n8)
charges against, 83
chosen as patriarch, 15–16,
18, 19
"confession/repentance" of,
84–85, 87–89, 98
counterrevolutionary
accusations against, viii,
71–72, 81–83, 89–90,
98 (*See also* "Living
Church" schism)
death of, viii, 22, 75, 103–6,
114

Decree No. 362 of, 51, 75, 79
as diocesan bishop, 23(n1)
Donskoy Monastery and
(*See* Donskoy
Monastery)
enthronement of, 18,
127(n19)
family of (*See* Bellavin, Vasily
Ivanovich)
fearlessness of, 87–88
first sermon as patriarch by,
18–19
funeral of, 105–6
GPU and (*See* GPU)
grave of, 117
Gregory VII and, 137–38(n17)
hospitalization of, 100–104
and innovations in church,
65, 132(n15)
letter to Eastern Orthodox
Patriarchs by, 54–55
letter to Supreme Court by,
84–85
lifestyle of, 3, 53
Living Church conference
and, 77, 78 (*See also*
"Living Church"
schism)
love of people in, 116
as martyr, 117
message after prison release
of, 90–95
as metropolitan of Moscow,
10–19, 115
monastic vows taken by, 3,
120–21(n12)
Moscow Council and, 11–19,
23–24

Chosen for His People